ISBN 978-1-334-01590-8
PIBN 10688455

This book is a reproduction of an important historical work. Forgotten Books uses
state-of-the-art technology to digitally reconstruct the work, preserving the original format
whilst repairing imperfections present in the aged copy. In rare cases, an imperfection in
the original, such as a blemish or missing page, may be replicated in our edition. We do,
however, repair the vast majority of imperfections successfully; any imperfections that
remain are intentionally left to preserve the state of such historical works.

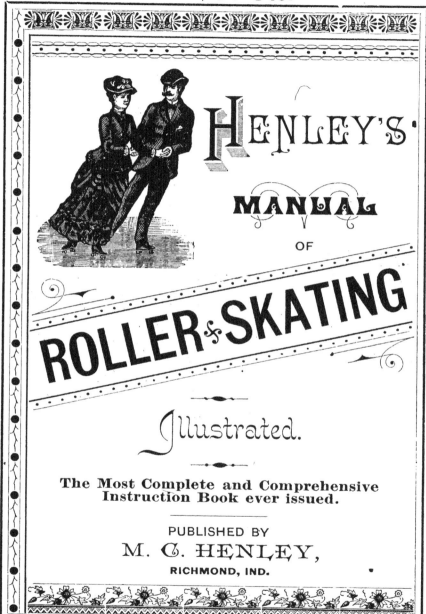

HENLEY'S

MANUAL

OF

ROLLER & SKATING

Illustrated.

The Most Complete and Comprehensive Instruction Book ever issued.

PUBLISHED BY

M. C. HENLEY,

RICHMOND, IND.

HENLEY'S

MANUAL OF

ROLLER SKATING

CONTAINING

OVER TWO HUNDRED ILLUSTRATIONS,

WITH

Complete Descriptions of all Movements Performed on
Roller Skates.

PUBLISHED BY

M. C. HENLEY,

ROLLER SKATE MANUFACTURER.

RICHMOND, INDIANA.

RICHMOND:
M. CULLATON & CO., PRINTERS AND BINDERS.
1885.

COPYRIGHT BY M. C. HENLEY,
1885.

PREFACE.

The amusements to which the people of a nation resort have such a potent influence upon the nation as a unit and the people as individuals, that we cannot afford to suffer evil amusements to exist or to neglect to foster good ones. Within the last few years roller skating has taken such a popular hold upon the people of this country that now there is a skating rink in every city and town, and even in villages of a few hundred inhabitants. All this is either a mighty influence for good or for bad.

There are those who are overworked; there are those who do not work at all. Men there may be who die without having known one day of real pleasure in their lives, who, even in childhood, had to work unceasingly to support themselves and perhaps some dear mother, or brother, or sister, and who, after having worked their way up into business, have contracted, as it were, a chronic habit and abnormal desire for money. On the other hand, there are those who have never known one day of honest work, people who have been raised in luxury until, surfeited with amusements that *are* beneficial, they seek gaming houses and places of drink. The peaceful tramp, if there be such an one, who has no care for the morrow, and who enjoys the rising and the setting of the sun, the rainy as well as the sunlit day, the starry or moonlight nights, and sundry marks on gate posts which indicate "good lunch," is to be envied rather than the millionaire who is so tied up in his business, literally a slave to it, that he never spends a day from it without fear of losing a fortune, and who cannot enjoy the evenings at home or in society because of ill health. Extreme overwork, we take it, is sinful as well as extreme indulgence of the desire for pleasure. Whatever tends to bring about the happy medium between these two extremes is certainly to be fostered and cherished as an institution necessary to a correct and permanent civilization.

We submit this book, therefore, with the feeling that it is not only an exponent of a fascinating art, but that it will be, in its way, one of the many influences for good.

CONTENTS.

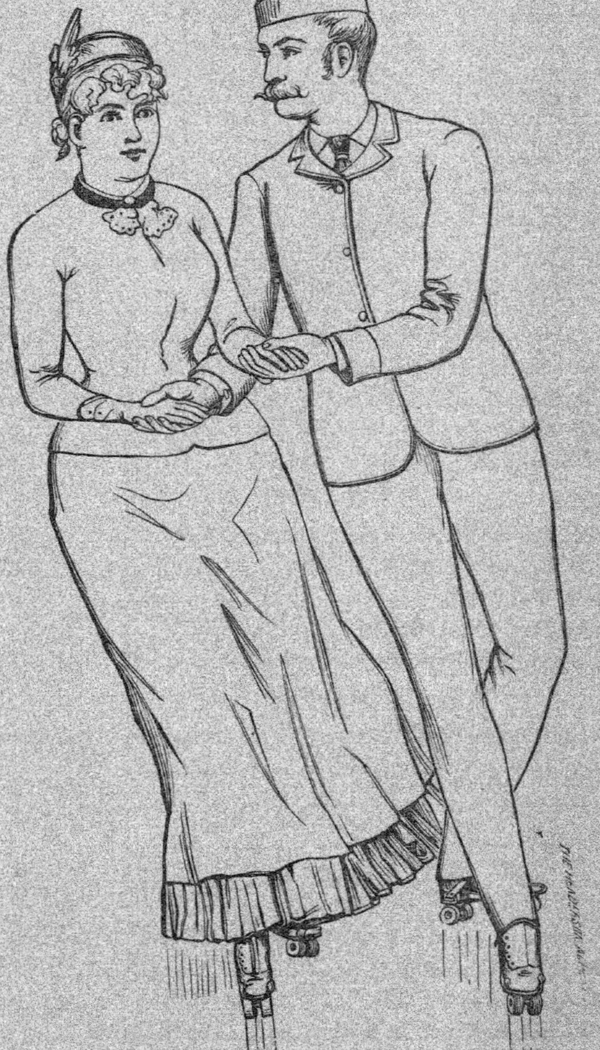

HENLEY'S MANUAL OF ROLLER SKATING.

CHAPTER I.

A BRIEF HISTORY OF SKATING.

THOUGH it appears to be impossible to fix on the time when skating first took root, there can be no doubt that it was introduced from more northern climates, where it originated more from the necessities of the inhabitants than as a pastime. When snow covered their land, and ice bound up their rivers, imperious necessity would soon suggest to the Scands or the Germans some ready means of winter locomotion. This first took the form of snow-shoes, with two long runners of wood, like those still used by the inhabitants of the northerly parts of Norway and Sweden in their journeys over the immense snow fields. These seem originally to have been used by the Finns, "for which reason," says a Swedish writer, "they were called 'Skrid Finnai,' (Sliding Finns,) a common name for the most ancient inhabitants of Sweden, both in the north Saga and by foreign authors. When used on ice, one runner would soon have been found more convenient than the widely separated two, and harder materials used than wood; first bone was substituted; then it, in turn, gave place to iron; and thus the present form of skate was developed in the North at a period set down by Scandinavian archæologists as about A. D. 200."

Frequent allusions occur in the old Northern poetry, which prove that proficiency in skating was one of the most highly esteemed accomplishments of the Northern heroes. One of them, named Kolson, boasts that he is master of nine accomplishments, skating being one ; while the hero, Harold, bitterly complains that though he could fight, ride, swim, glide along the ice on skates, dart the lance, and row, " yet a Russian maid disdains me."

In the " Edda " this accomplishment is singled out for special praise : " Then the king asked what that young man could do who accompanied Thor. Thialfe answered that in running upon skates he would dispute the prize with any of the courtiers. The king owned that the talent he spoke of was a very fine one."

Olaus Magnus, the author of the famous chapter in the Snakes of Iceland, tells us that skates were made " of polished iron, or of the shank-bone of a deer or sheep, about a foot long, filed down on one side, and greased with hog's lard to repel the wet." These rough-and-ready bone skates were the kind first adopted by the English ; for Fitzstephen, in his description of amusements of the Londoners in his day, (time of Henry II.,) tells us that " when that great fen that washes Moorfields at the north wall of the city is frozen over, great companies of young men go to sport upon the ice. Some, striding as wide as they may, do slide swiftly; some, better practiced to the ice, bind to their shoes bones, as the legs of some beasts, and hold stakes in their hands, headed with sharp iron, which sometimes they strike against the ice; these men go swiftly as doth a bird in the air, or a bolt from a cross-bow." Then he goes on to say that some, imitating the fashion of the tournament, would start in full career against one another, armed with poles; "they meet, elevate their poles, attack, and strike each other, when one or both of them fall, and not without some bodily hurt."

Specimens of these old bone skates are occasionally dug up in fenny parts of Great Britain. There are some in the British Museum, in the Museum of the Scottish Antiquaries, and probably in other collections; though, perhaps, some of the "finds" are not nearly as old as Fitzstephen's day, for there seems to be good evidence that even in London the primitive bone skate was not entirely superseded by implements of steel at the latter part of last century.

One found about 1839 in Moorfields, in the boggy soil peculiar to that district, is described as being formed of the bone of some animal, made smooth on one side, with a hole at one extremity for a cord to fasten it to the shoe. At the other end a hole is also drilled horizontally to a depth of three inches, which might have received a plug, with another cord to secure it more effectually.

There is hardly a greater difference between these old bone skates and the "acmes" and club skates of to-day, than there is between the skating of middle ages and the artistic and graceful movements of good performers of to-day. Indeed, skating as a fine art is entirely a thing of modern growth. Messrs. Vanderwell and Witham, authors of "A System of Figure Skating," "affirm from long experience and very close observation that, in spite of mild winters, the art has gone on improving up to the present time." This has often been denied, and many are the wonderful feats of renowned skaters of the past cited in support of this denial. Benjamin West, the President of the Academy, it is said, could trace with his skates on the ice the outlines of any statue that might be named. The Chevalier De St. George could sign his name upon the ice with the blade of his skate; while Strutt speaks of skaters "readily describing upon the ice the form of all the letters in the alphabet."

"Who has not heard," says Mr. Vanderwell, "from many old skaters of a generation that is fast fading away how some famous skater of their day cut his name, and who has not brought down their ire if the possibility of the feat was doubted?   *   *   *   It is most strange, but no less strange than true, that this feat, (except by standing on one foot and scraping the ice into resemblance of letters with the other,) is an impossibility either in ancient or modern skating."

The writer's observation would confirm the above, for of all the many expert ice skaters personally known, none have ever claimed the ability to perform the feat mentioned, and a careful reading of the movements of a Haines, or a Curtis, fail to show such as a listed movement. As "distance lends enchantment," so time enhances the "it may be" wonderful skating of a past into a phenomenal performance, but like a mirage, 'tis ever in the distance.

Much controversy still leaves unsettled the date of the first skate with wheels. Some go so far as to claim their use by the Romans during "Carnival Week." Others have it that their first use was in the presentation of one of Tom Hood's plays, in the year 1743, at the old Drury Lane Theater, London. Roller skates were also used at the Grand Opera House, Paris, durring the first representation of one of Meyerbeer's earlier operas.

It is safe to say that a skate with wheels was first used in this country by the "Ravels," a French family of acrobats, who made a tour of the larger cities some forty years ago. No greater difference can exist between the bone skate of Fitzstephen's time and the present steel skate than there does between the skate used by the Ravels and the present skate with wheels. Nor can the writer imagine a greater difference between the slide of the "Finn" and the graceful movements of the present ice skater, than there is between the ease and grace of our present roller skater and the skating of the Ravels. The construction of the skate (if such it can be called) of their day, necessarily prohibiting the artistic curve and grace so easily acquired on the skate now in common use, and their work was entirely of a muscular and acrobatic character.

Roller skating, as a fine art, is of very modern growth. For, as like those who give to ancient Egypt and Greece a higher civilization than that we now enjoy, so many in the art of skating accredit to the past a higher proficiency than that of the present, it being the habit of some to appreciate that which they have never seen more than that which they see. Being infatuated with the legends of the past, they are blind to the merit of the present, and the writer believes he voices the views of many who, though not unappreciative of the good performances of the skater of to-day, yet believe that the roller skater has not reached the "acme" of his art, and that the skater of the coming generation need not fail of hope to surpass in artistic skill the skater of the past or present.

CHAPTER II.

GENERAL REMARKS ON ROLLER SKATING.

VALUE OF HEALTH.

Health is one of the foundation pillars of happiness. It is an essential preliminary to the best success in profession, business, or society. Few people realize the importance of it until reminded by lack of it, and still fewer have any idea that exercise properly taken is often the ONLY means of securing and preserving it; while on the other hand patent medicine manufacturers are amassing fortunes.

J. Dorman Steele, M. D., in his valuable work on Physiology and Hygiene, says: "The body is the instrument which the mind uses. If it be dulled or nicked, the effect of the best labor will be impaired. The grandest gifts of mind or fortune are comparatively valueless unless there be a healthy body to use and enjoy them. The tramp, sturdy and brave with his outdoor life, is really happier than the rich man in his palace with the gout to twinge him amid his pleasures. The day has gone by when delicacy was considered necessarily an element of beauty. Weakness is timid and irresolute; strength is full of force and energy."

Physical health is necessary to mental health, and *vice versa*. The mental health cannot be impaired without impairing the physical. Physical health is valuable to the brain worker. Mental health is valuable to the manual worker.

Health is positively essential to the highest degree of beauty to which a person is capable of attaining. Health insures a clear, rich complexion, bright eyes, and an active mind with which to entertain and be entertained.

EXERCISE NECESSARY TO HEALTH.

Even the slight exercise of dressing, eating, and walking keeps those of sedentary habits in as good health as they are; for if a person should take to his bed for six or eight weeks, although there be no sickness, he would be so enfeebled that, at the end of that time, he could scarcely walk.

J. C. Dalton, M. D., in his work on Physiology and Hygiene, says: "It is very important that the muscles should be trained and exercised by sufficient daily use. Too much confinement by sedentary occupations, in study, or by simple indulgence in indolent habits, will certainly impair the strength of the body and injuriously affect the health; and this exercise cannot be neglected with impunity any more than the due provision of clothing and food." J. D. Steele, in his work above referred to, also says: "No education is complete which fails to provide for the development of the muscles. Were gymnastics or calisthenics as regular an exercise as grammar or arithmetic, fewer pupils would be compelled to leave school on account of ill health; while weak bodies and ungraceful gaits would no longer characterize so many of our best institutions." And again the same author says: "The blood contains the materials for the making of every organ. Where there is work to be done or repairs to be made, there oxygen is needed. Exercise actually burns out parts of the muscles and other tissues as wood is burned in a stove; and the blood when foul with the refuse of this fire, is whirled back to the lungs where it is purified, giving off the poisons gathered up in its circulation and absorbing the oxygen of the air." Where exercise tears down, nature always endeavors to build anew with better and more material in order to make the part, whether muscle, brain, or bone, stronger and more fitted for doing its peculiar work.

AMUSEMENT NECESSARY TO HEALTH.

The desire for amusement is as natural as the desire for food, and must be indulged as well. It is necessary that we relax our minds and bodies at various intervals and take recreation of some kind. Mirth is a nerve tonic. Dalton, above referred to, says: "The digestion of the food is much influenced by the *condition of the nervous system*. Every one is aware how readily any anxiety, anger, or vexation will take away the appetite and interfere with digestion." Is it not of primary importance that our food be digested well?

SKATING AS A SUPERIOR EXERCISE.

The reader may have asked why we dwell so earnestly upon health and exercise in a roller skating manual. It is because roller skating very greatly benefits or injures the health, according to its proper or careless indulgence. It can be made a splendid blessing, but like all other amusements it may be made the means of much harm. But comparing skating on even terms with other amusements, we are of the opinion that it is superior to all of them, roller skating especially. It gives to every muscle in the body more or less activity. There is no extraordinary strain upon any one muscle, but a pleasurable tension of every muscle. The blood does not flow to one particular part to strengthen it, but to every portion, strengthening the whole body. Of course this kind of exercise may be indulged in to exhaustion just as well as dancing. As to the proper amount of skating at one time we give instructions elsewhere. The mind is most thoroughly taken away from every thought of the business world, and for the while, at least, is free from care. The mind is taken up with the rink, the skating movements, the skaters, and perhaps some interesting partner. When the skater becomes at home on the skates, he can execute movements so airy and graceful that he feels almost as if he could fly. In fact the motions are nearer to those of a bird in flight than anything else performed by man.

Salzman, in his valuable work on exercise, says, in reference to skating: "I am come to an exercise superior to everything that can be classed under the head of motion. I know of nothing in gymnastics that displays equal elegance as skating. It excites such pleasure in the mind of the performer that I should recommend it as the most efficacious remedy to the misanthrope and hypochondriac."

Campe, writing in reference to the same subject, says: "I know not of a more pleasant or beneficial exercise, and every child, boy or girl, ought to learn it." And he might have added with equal truth, "every man or woman.

Dalton says: "A special increase of strength may be produced to a very great extent by the constant practice or training of particular muscles; but the best condition is that in which all the different organs and systems of the body have their full and complete development, no one of them preponderating excessively over the others."

Another authority says: "Skating sends the blood to the surface of the body in healthy circulation, and by rousing the dormant functions of the skin, relieves the overworked internal organs and gives new life and vigor to the general system. This naturally affects the mental powers beneficially, and with restored health the ill nature incident to a disordered body, and the bad feelings engendered by a neglected physique, disappear to be superseded by the natural feelings of a healthy person. If you wish to realize the truth of this, visit some of the large skating rinks, and watch the pleasant smile of the rosy-cheeked girl on skates, and listen to the gay laugh of beginners as well as experts, and contrast these effects with the serious manner and pale countenance of the over-housed girl and the languid movements of the office-confined clerk, and you will then see what a gain it is to indulge in such healthy recreative amusement.'

Skating induces a graceful carriage; expands the chest; teaches self-reliance. In the effort to avoid collision, it trains the mind and eye to quick action.

THE ROLLER SKATING RINK.

If the foregoing be true of ice skating, how much more ought it to be emphasized in regard to roller skating. Most all of the rinks of to-day have all the modern conveniences. It is only necessary to think of the ice skating years ago, of the frozen fingers, cold toes, no resting without catching cold, the long walk to and from the lake, pond, or river, treacherous air-holes, dangerous snags, etc.

Compare this with the roller rink of the present, with its electric lights, music, and many conveniences. Be it in the land of ice-locked lake or river, or under the genial Southern sun, where rivers and brooks run on through all seasons without knowing the winter's cold, we now skate free from the attendant discomforts and oftentime fatal exposure of the old-time skating above mentioned

MORAL VIEW OF THE SKATING RINK.

In many of the amusements of to-day there is too much of an element of chance and a strong desire to win. People who really know better, do sometimes quarrel over a game of cards, croquet, lawn tennis, dominoes, or some other game, while about the only element of chance there is in skating as indulged by the general public is the chance of falling, and very often quite enough of this element to make it interesting. As for disputes, there are no occasions for them. Bishop McTyeir, in a letter to the *Christian Advocate*, writes : "Allow me to commend to you and your readers roller skating. It can and should substitute dancing as an exercise and amusement for the young people of both sexes. It furnishes indoor, lively, graceful exercise, both muscular and nervous excitement, and leaves no excuse for dancing. I wish there was a skating rink in every village and boarding school." Since the writing of this letter, his wish has been nearly if not quite fully realized; and not only the young people, but the older ones, fathers and mothers, are learning and enjoying the splendid privileges to which the invention of the roller skate has brought us. We quote again from the *Ladies' Boudoir:* "As a fashionable exercise for ladies, there is nothing so well adapted to the development and display of a fine figure as roller skating; and in no way can a lady present equal elegance and grace as when circling about on skates. The accomplishment is becoming a very important part of every young lady's education." A learned and noted divine of Louisville writes : "Roller skating is just the thing wanted by our young people, especially the girls. It affords just the sort of exercise they require for their physical development— gentle but active, and so attractive that they cannot resist it. It is my deliberate opinion that no conception has entered the mind of mortal in this century so important to the health of our girls in our cities, as this skating *indoors*."

The rinks have come to stay. They have been built or are being built in every town of a few hundred in- habitants; and the thousands of traveling men, sales- men and business men, men traveling for pleasure, now know where to go in a strange city without going to a saloon or billiard hall in order to pass away an hour or two. There are instances known where the rinks have injured the saloon business so that the sa- loon keepers want the rinks taxed. What does this in- dicate? This is not a temperance work, but when it comes to comparing the good which twenty-five cents worth of liquor does with the good which twenty-five cents worth of skating does, we are emphatically in favor of the skating rink. The rinks are a vast and potent influence, and are taking an important part in our moral economies. They are more powerful for good than statute books or lectures—we had almost said sermons. They persuade but do not coerce. The invention of the roller skate is more of a blessing to mankind than the invention of the telegraph, for the former brings health and happiness directly and indi- rectly, while the telegraph can only aid us indirectly.

SKATING CLUBS.

We would recommend the organization of skating clubs wherever feasible. They would be especially use- ful in the advancement of combination skating, such as marches, may-poles, combination eighths, etc. If properly conducted, they tend more to the advancement of the art than any other means which can be adopted. The spirit of emulation is ever present, and is quite an inducement to improvement. By observation we learn more rapidly than by any other mode. We may be able to learn from others movements we do not yet know, and we may be able to teach them in return movements which they have not yet learned. In many of our smaller towns a large club might rent the rink one night in every week with but small proportional expense. Instructors, floor managers, leaders of the march might be elected every month, as well as officers that are common to all societies. We hope for the success of all skating clubs.

CHAPTER III.

HYGIENE OF THE RINK.

HOW TO CATCH COLD.

It must be remembered that when exercising the body requires very light clothing, and the same is especially true of skating. If heavy clothing be worn, the body becomes uncomfortably warm in a short time, and an open window or cool draught is quite a temptation; but if the clothing be light an additional garment can be thrown around the shoulders when resting without any discomfort. Flannel is excellent worn next the skin, as it absorbs the perspiration better than any other material, and those who frequent the rink should positively wear it so.

Steele says, in regard to the subject of colds: "The skin is chilled and the perspiration is checked. The blood, no longer cleansed and reduced in volume by the drainage through the pores, sets to the lungs for purification. That organ is oppressed, breathing becomes difficult, and the *extra secretion* by the irritated surface of the mucous membrane is thrown off by coughing. The mucous membrane of the nasal chamber sympathizes with the difficulty, and we have a 'cold in the head.' In general the excess of blood is very great when the pores of the skin are suddenly closed, and goes to the weakest point, developing in some people pleurisy, in others pneumonia, in others quick consumption, etc. WHERE ONE PERSON HAS BEEN KILLED IN BATTLE, THOUSANDS HAVE DIED OF COLDS."

HOW TO CURE A COLD.

The same author further says: "The excess of blood goes to the weak points and there produces congestion. To withdraw the blood from the congested part and free the blood from the poisons it ought to have given off in the form of perspiration, should be the object of all treatment. Medicines will not do it. Hot foot baths have saved multitudes of lives. It is well in case of a sudden cold to go immediately to bed, and with hot drinks and extra clothing, open the pores, induce free perspiration, and bring the blood from the congested portion to the surface of the body. The rule for the prevention and cure of a cold is to *keep the blood upon the surface.*"

AVOID EXHAUSTION.

Never skate until exhausted. Exercise to be beneficial must always stop short of fatigue. If the limbs are so tired at night that you cannot sleep, then you have skated too much; or, if by tapping the muscles that are used most in skating you find they ache, then you have skated too much. This is a sure test, whether you have skated but three minutes or three hours. A beginner, from the very nature of things, becomes tired in much less time than an experienced skater with muscles well developed. You can soon learn to gauge the amount of skating you ought to do by the effect upon the muscles and the nervous system the day after. The novice must skate but very little at first and gradually increase the amount of skating at one time so as to give the muscles time to grow and strengthen.

Quoting from Dalton again: "It will not do for any person to remain inactive during the greater part of the week and then take an excessive amount of exercise on a single day. An unnatural deficiency of this kind cannot be compensated by an occasional excess. Exercise which is so violent and continued as to produce exhaustion or unnatural fatigue is an injury instead of an advantage, and creates a waste and expenditure of the muscular force instead of its healthy increase.

AVOID TIGHT LACING.

This precaution seems to address itself so plainly to the common sense of every one that we had thought of omitting it, but we might say in this connection to those who *do* know of the pernicious effects of tight lacing, especially when skating, and yet persist in not heeding the above suggestion, that they should lace still tighter. It is the "fool-killer's" way. Those who read this and feel guilty will no doubt throw away this book in disgust. But speaking seriously, we would say that skating, like all exercise, requires deeper and faster breathing than when the body is in normal action. If the lungs are not allowed to inflate to the fullest extent that nature involuntarily demands, the blood is not purified fast enough and poisons are left in it to pass through the system again and induce the headache.   Stooping shoulders are not elegant or healthful.

AVOID ICE-WATER.

A very intelligent and distinguished physician says: "Drinks should be sipped and not gulped. Very few who have indulged in the rapid drinking of ice-water have failed to notice that a sudden pain in the head was the result. It may have been a sharp shoot, or a mere feeling of dullness, and it may have passed off in a moment, but it was at least incipient congestion of the brain." There are other evils attendant upon the drinking of ice-water. Cool water, but not ice-water, should be provided at all rinks. If only ice-water is to be had at the rink, wait until you reach home. This rule is very important.

NEVER skate immediately after eating. At least an hour should intervene between meal time and skating.

Wait in the skate room or hall before going into the out-door air if it be very cold, until the breathing becomes normal.

WALK HOME.—If the distance will permit, walk home by all means, and walk briskly, too, briskly enough to keep warm.

Change underclothing immediately upon reaching home. It should never in any case be allowed to dry upon the person.

POSITION OF THE BODY

Keep the body erect, the shoulders back, and the head up. Do not sway the weight forward by bending the small of the back or at the hips. The body must be kept straight and bent forward from the ankle. Bend the limbs but very slightly at the knee. At the commencement of each stroke the knee of the performing leg should be flexed and then gradually straightened, but not rigidly. The feet should always be kept near each other. In plain skating the balance foot should never leave the floor more than half an inch or an inch. Learn from the very first to hold the arms still. If the stroke is right there is no tendency to swing the arm. It is better to hold the arms rigidly at the side than to allow them to fly around in the air promiscuously as if they were grasping at straws.

ONE-SIDEDNESS.

The great majority of people are right-sided; a few are left-sided, while still fewer are equally right-sided or left-sided. Just why this is so is not here necessary to explain, but that it is the cause of unsymmetrical figures and ungraceful gaits is a fact. We quote from Prof. Walker in his valuable work on Exercise for Ladies· "The one-sidedness with which nearly all the acts of life are performed is the general cause of the greatest and most universal deformity which can only be prevented by an equal and similar use of the other side." We call attention to this fact because the natural tendency of skaters is generally to use the right foot in preference and to the neglect of the left. If the right foot be used ever so skillfully and the left foot awkwardly, the skating will be imperfect and ungraceful. Very few even of our expert skaters are able to execute with as much precision and grace a figure or movement upon the left foot which they can perform perfectly upon the right. Yet there is no excuse for this one-sidedness. To remedy the fault it only requires practice upon the weaker side, whether it be right or left side. The habitual neglect of the left foot will surely hinder the progress of the skater and prevent him from performing many figures which call for an equal use and skill of either foot. The beginner should avoid this fault from the very first. Practice on the left all the more if there is an inclination to neglect it.

Continually going around the rink to the left is a very great mistake of the management of the rinks, and those who refuse to skate to the right, which comes under the head of one-sidedness. Exactly one-half of the skating time of every rink should be spent in going around to the right; and gentlemen skating with ladies should always be on the inside, that is, when going to the left, be on the left of the lady, and when going to the right, be on the right of the lady. An equal proficiency in skating to the right or to the left is positively necessary to even those who only expect to become good "plain" skaters. As we said before, to correct this deficiency is only a matter of practice. There are those who are ambidextrous; in fact, ambidexterity is taught in many of our best business colleges, while in the larger cities may be found book-keepers who write equally as well with the right or with the left hand.

RAPIDITY INCOMPATIBLE WITH GRACE.

Rapidity may be very essential and desirable in the business world, in races, or railroading, but it is thoroughly incompatible with grace of movement in skating. A graceful movement must be made without effort, or at least apparent effort. A fast movement cannot be performed without effort and apparent effort. Our most artistic and graceful skaters are light in their movements without rapidity. Although the majority of skaters skate as though they were practicing for a race, please do not do likewise. Grace of movement is one of the essentials of good skating. There must be no angular movements, positions, shuffling, or scrambling. Haste is sure to cause bad habits which can never be entirely eradicated. In plain skating especially every movement should be a curve. Curves are lines of beauty. A person may learn to skate fast without learning to make even one graceful movement. Prof. Alvaro, an authority on exercise, says concerning grace of movement: "Remember it takes some muscle to move the body or limbs with perfect grace. The circus performer, as airy and light as he appears, cannot go through his exercise gracefully until his muscles are so developed that he peforms with ease what another cannot perform at all. To the ladies we would say: 'Don't be afraid of a little muscle. It will take a very great deal to take the beautiful curves out of the contour of the body and limbs, and in fact, with a great many, it will take a great deal to bring those curves there.'" We wish to emphasize the fact that rapidity is not grace by saying that many of our good skaters skate two to three times as fast as they ought.

HOW TO PRACTICE.

Learn one thing at a time. Do not pass from one movement to another until you have learned to execute the first perfectly every time you try it. Petulant haste to learn all the movements in one evening will only result in learning nothing. The first movements are very essential in all skating, and should therefore be studied and practiced with great care and deliberation. The first movements are to be found somewhere in nearly all fancy skating. They cannot be neglected if you wish to learn quickly and well. In learning, practice a little at a time and as often as possible.

DRESS.

Flapping coat-skirts, baggy pantaloons, long dresses, and hoop-skirts are decidedly out of place when skating. The costume should be trim and neat. Very thin, narrow, or high-heeled shoes should never be worn. Beginners should wear longer skates than experienced skaters. The skate for a beginner should be long enough to bring the front rollers an inch or an inch and a half forward of the ball of the foot. But as he becomes more expert, he may shorten them until the front rollers come directly under the ball of the foot.

CHAPTER IV.

THE ELEMENTARY PRINCIPLES.

There are twelve elementary principles, one or more of which enter into any and every movement performed on skates. They are as follows:

1. The Roll.
2. The Compound Curve.
3. The Lap-foot.
4. Change of heel and toe.
5. Pivot-foot.
6. Reverse foot.
7. The Extra push.
8. The Polka step.
9. The Turn.
10. The Halt foot.
11. The Split.
12. The Whirl.

We shall proceed to define each principle in a general way, after which we will take up special illustrations of each and their variations.

THE ROLL.

This is the first and most essential principle to learn. It necessarily forms a part of all skating. It is a stroke, or glide, generally curving more or less to the right or to the left. The straight rolls are not so graceful as the curved ones. Every curved roll should be an arc of a circle and not of an ellipse, oval, or para-bola. (See Fig. 1.) The weight must be swayed or thrown directly towards the other end of the roll, as represented by the dotted line AB, and not in the direc-tion indicated by the toe at the commencement of the stroke, as represented by the dotted line AC. During the greater part of the length of the roll the body leans towards the center of the arc at D, the centrifugal force bringing the body up in position to be swayed in the direction of the end of the next or new roll. The head describes the curve AEB.

THE COMPOUND CURVE.

This is simply joining two rolls of opposite curva-ture, as in Fig. 2. The line described by the head in performing this compound roll or curve is represented by the dotted line AC, the body coming to a perpen-dicular position at B, and again at C.

THE LAP-FOOT.

This principle is used in all cross rolls and lap-foot circles. It is simply carrying one foot around in front of or behind the other foot and placing it down to the outside, as in Figs. 3 and 4. In the cross rolls, each foot is lapped over the other alternately, while in lap-foot circle to the left, the right foot is continually lap-ped over the left. In lap-foot circle to the right, the left foot is continually lapped over the right.

THE CHANGE OF HEEL AND TOE.

There are six modifications of this principle : change from heel to toe, change from toe to heel, change from flat foot to heel, change from heel to flat foot, change from flat foot to toe, and change from toe to flat foot. Examples : A roll may be started on the flat foot and changed to toe, that is, finished on the toe ; or the roll may be started on the heel and finished on the toe, etc.

PIVOT-FOOT.

This is holding one foot still as a center or pivot while the other foot circles around, or partly around it. The pivot-foot must be rested on the heel or toe, and not on the flat foot. The weight is necessarily borne pretty well on the inside of the skate of the circle foot, or outside, as the case may be, so that the circle foot will make a small arc or circle. Pivot-foot is used in eights or threes, or in turning from forward to backward, or backward to forward.

THE REVERSE FOOT.

This principle includes seven modifications, or special variations, as follows :

Fig. 5. Spread-eagle Reverse foot.
" 6. Pivot Reverse foot.
" 7. Cut-off Reverse foot.
" 8. Side-step Reverse foot.
" 9. Dizzy No. 1 Reverse foot.
" 10. Dizzy No. 2 Reverse foot.
" 11. The Toe-turn Reverse foot.

In the illustrations of Reverse foot, the left foot is the reverse foot. The same variations may also be executed with the right foot.

Figs. 6 and 10 may be used alternately in a field movement which would cause the body to turn constantly to the left.

Fig. 7, using the left foot as reverse foot, and Fig. 10, using the right foot as reverse foot, may be used in combination for a field movement, keeping the body facing one way and making a series of inside rolls on the left foot and compound rolls on the right foot, and so on. For the other combinations see List of Field Movements.

THE EXTRA PUSH.

This is, as the name indicates, simply an extra push with the foot that has just left the floor. It will be readily understood by referring to the illustration, Fig. 12.

THE POLKA-STEP.

The Polka-step breaks each roll up into short strokes, giving to the movement a rythmic beat, which may be performed to music.

THE TURN.

This is performed by keeping the toe on the floor while the heel is lifted slightly and turned to the right or to the left; or, by keeping the heel on the floor and lifting the toe slightly and turning it to the right or to the left. The turn will be readily understood by examining the illustrations.

THE HALT FOOT.

This is performed by turning the foot up on the toe so that the front rollers and the toe of the shoe will rest on the floor, as in the toe-stops, but instead of allowing the foot to slide along and gradually stop, the foot is stopped suddenly while the body passes on and the next foot assumes stroke position.

THE SPLIT.

This is made by first taking standing position and allowing the feet to take diverging strokes, or rolls, as represented in Fig. 13, and also in Fig. 14.

THE WHIRL.

A whirl is one complete turn of the body. A spin is a continued whirl. Whirls and spins may be performed upon one foot or two feet, but never flat foot. Two foot whirls are generally made on the heel of one foot and the toe of the other foot. Spins may be started either with pivot foot circle, (see Fig. 15,) or splits. (See Fig. 16.)

CHAPTER V.

THE GENERAL VARIATIONS.

There are nine general variations, all of which are applicable to most movements. Those variations which are peculiar to certain movements are called special variations. The general variations are as follows ·

1. Forward.
2. Backward.
3. Outside Roll.
4. Inside Roll.
5. Right.
6. Left.
7. Flat-foot.
8. Heel.
9. Toe.

That is, for instance, a roll may be performed forward making an outside roll, on the right foot, and on the flat-foot; or it may be made on the left toe, backward, making an inside roll, etc.

We now proceed to the specific movements.

A good bird's-eye view of the subject may be gained by studying the following outlines :

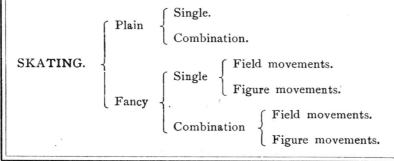

PLAIN.
- Single.
- Combination.
  - The plain outside roll, forw. and backw.
  - The plain inside roll, " "
  - The lap-foot circle to the left.
  - The lap-foot circle to the right.

FANCY SINGLE. (Field.)
- Continuous
  - Two foot movements.
  - One foot movements.
- Broken
  - Two foot movements.
  - One foot movements.

FANCY SINGLE. (Figure.)
- Continuous
  - Two foot movements.
  - One foot movements.
- Broken
  - Two foot movements.
  - One foot movements.

FANCY SINGLE CONTINUOUS FIELD MOVEMENTS.
- Two-foot
  - Skulls.
  - Serpentines.
  - Zigzags.
  - Spread-eagles.
  - Guide foot rolls.
  - Pivot-foot rolls.
  - Mercuries.
  - Flying turns.
  - Flying whirls.
  - Grapevines.
- One-foot
  - Serpentines.
  - Zigzags.
  - Mercuries.
  - Flying threes.
  - Locomotives.
  - Grapevines.

FANCY SINGLE
BROKEN
FIELD MOVEMENTS.

Two-foot
- Plain outside backward.
- Plain inside backward.
- Changes of roll.
- Cross rolls.
- Extra push rolls.
- Lock-foot rolls.
- Halt-foot rolls.
- Reverse-foot rolls.
- Toe-whirl rolls.
- Heel-whirl rolls.
- Flying threes.

One-foot
- Changes of roll.
- Toe-whirl rolls.
- Flying threes.
- Hop-rolls.

FANCY SINGLE FIGURES.

Continuous and Broken.
- Circles.
- Eights.
- Threes.
- Fives.
- Squares.
- Hexagons.
- Splits.
- Scissors.
- Spins.
- Whirls.

PLAIN COMBINATION.
- Plain outside roll.
- Plain inside roll.
- Lap-foot circle to the left.
- Lap-foot circle to the right.

FANCY COMBINATION.
- Long roll, alternating sides.
- Flying Scud.
- Mercury.
- And other movements, according to the proficiency of the skaters.
- The March.
- The May-pole.
- Eights.
- Circles.

CHAPTER VI.

PLAIN SINGLE, OR INSTRUCTIONS TO BEGINNERS.

THE OUTSIDE ROLL.

The word "Roll," as used here and hereafter, has reference to the movement as a whole, and not to any particular stroke, as used heretofore. This outside roll is the one most used in skating, whether single, fancy, or combination. It is much prettier than the inside roll. It is the first movement for the beginner to learn, and to that end we give the following seven lessons:

Lesson 1. Take standing position, (Fig. 17,) with the heel of the right foot touching the hollow of the left and the greater part of the weight borne on the left foot. Change from this to the other standing position, (Fig. 18,) by first changing the weight from the left to the right and then placing the heel of the left foot to the hollow of the right. Then transfer the weight of the body to the left and place the heel of the right to the hollow of the left again. Make this change several times until you feel quite secure in the execution of it, and the body will have advanced by a series of short steps as represented in Fig 6. During the performance of this movement the feet should be kept perfectly level; that is, do not allow them to rock from side to side. The ankle must be held stiff while learning to skate, so as not to allow the foot to bear on one side of the skate more than on the other. If you do not already have a graceful carriage, now is the time to acquire it. Learn to skate gracefully, and you will be graceful in your gait on the street or in the home. The body and head should be held erect, the shoulders back, and the arms hanging easily down at the side. It is much better, however, to hold the arms stiffly down at the side than to allow them to catch the air for support. Neither the performing leg or balance leg should ever be straightened rigidly, but always more or less bent at the knee. On the other hand, be very careful to allow the knee to bend but slightly. The body should never be inclined forward by bending at the hips, or stooping of the shoulders, or bending the head down to look at the feet, or all of these combined. In plain skating the feet should always be kept as close to each other as possible.

Lesson 2. Same as Lesson 1, except place the feet at the angle indicated in Fig. 23. The weight of the body should be principally borne on the front rollers. Remember to keep the feet level.

. *Lesson* 3. Same as Lesson 2, except allow the skate to roll two or three inches, thus making a series of short strokes as represented in Fig. 24. Each stroke should be of exactly the same length. If the feet have been kept level, the strokes thus far will be perfectly straight.

Lesson 4. Same as Lesson 3, except take a little

longer stroke, about eight or ten inches. Remember
the weight should be borne mostly on the front rollers.

Lesson 5. Gradually increase the length of stroke
as taken in the preceding lesson to three or four feet
in length, keeping the feet level and making a straight
stroke.

Lesson 6. Same as Lesson 5, except bear very
slightly on the outside of the skate, which will cause
the stroke to curve to the outside as in Fig. 25. Remember that you should not push on the foot which
just leaves the floor so as to gain momentum. This is
acquired by swaying the body forward towards the
other end of the stroke to be taken.

Lesson 7. Gradually increase the length of the
stroke as taken in Lesson 6 until you can make each
one fifteen or twenty feet long. During the performance of a stroke or roll, the balance foot is properly
carried by keeping the hollow of it at the heel of the
floor foot, the toe pointing slightly downwards within
half an inch or an inch of the floor. Just a little before
the completion of the stroke the balance foot is brought
around to stroke position; that is, with the heel of the
balance foot at the hollow of the floor foot. See Fig.
26. The line described by the head is a serpentine as
represented by the dotted line, in which there must be
no angles.

THE INSIDE ROLL.

This is really the "Dutch Roll," although many call
the lap-foot front cross roll the "Dutch Roll" by mis-

take. The inside roll should be learned next after the outside roll.

Lesson 8. This is the same as Lesson 6, but instead of bearing the weight on the outside of the skate it should now be borne slightly on the inside, which will cause the stroke to curve to the inside as in Fig. 27.

Lesson 9. Gradually increase the length of the stroke as learned in Lesson 8 to fifteen or twenty feet. Observe directions as to balance foot given in Lesson 7. Observe also all directions as to position of body, etc. See Fig. 28. The dotted line represents the line described by the head.

LAP-FOOT CIRCLE TO THE LEFT.

Lesson 10. Cut a circle to the left by making an outside roll with the left foot and an inside roll with the right foot, bring the right foot around in front and placing it down to the left of the left foot as represented in Fig. 29.

LAP-FOOT CILCLE TO THE RIGHT.

Lesson 11. Cut a circle to the right by making an outside roll with the right foot and an inside roll with the left foot, bring the left foot around in front of and placing it down to the right of the right foot as represented in Fig. 30.

The lap-foot as performed in these two circles is called the lap-foot front. See Fig. 3.

When the foregoing eleven lessons are thoroughly learned, the march may then be attempted with confidence. The outside roll and the lap-foot circle movement, which is used in turning sharp corners, are by far the two movements used most in skating. The outside roll is the prettiest field movement performed on skates. It is the one used most in combination skating, and is in itself alone well worth the time and trouble to learn it. A march, unless the participants have learned some other movements, should include only these four movements.

CHAPTER VII.

FANCY SINGLE. — CONTINUOUS TWO-FOOT FIELD MOVEMENTS.

SKULLS.

In Fig. 31 the pushes or pressure is made with each foot alternately as shown by the shaded portions of either line. The flat-foot skulls are not as pretty or fancy as some other movements, but are quite necessary to learn in order to get the compound curve in the changes of roll perfectly. When performed on the heels or toes, toes especially, they are very showy. In Fig. 32 the pushes are made simultaneously. Perfection in this movement will be of great advantage in learning and performing many other movements. When the feet come nearest together they should almost touch, and when they separate, should not separate more than eighteen or twenty inches.

Fig. 33 is much prettier than the other two, and should be practiced well. Each foot passes alternately in front of the other. For example, when the feet approach, let the right pass ahead and cross in front of the left; but the next time the left passes ahead and in front of the right, etc.

When Fig. 31 is performed on the heels or toes, each foot should pass ahead of the other more than when performed flat-foot.

SERPENTINES.

Fig. 34. The toe of the rear foot should touch the heel of the front foot. The motion is sustained by the swaying of the body from side to side in such a way as to jerk the body forward. Should be practiced until it can be performed so gracefully that the swaying of the body is so slight that it does not have the appearance of giving impetus to it. Learn this movement on heels and toes as well as flat-foot; it is used in some very pretty figure eights.

ZIGZAGS.

Fig. 35. This is learned by first placing the heels together and toes pointed out at right angles to each other. Lift the heel of the right foot and the toe of the left foot, carrying them, the heel and toe so lifted, to the right until the toes are together and the heels separated. Then lift the toe of the right foot and the heel of the left foot, carrying the toe and heel so lifted again to the right, which will bring the feet into the same position as assumed at first. Continue this simple movement until it is performed easily, and then attempt the figure by moving the right foot from b to f. and the left foot from c to d simultaneously, but passing the right foot in front of the left at the crossing a. Then make a toe turn with the left foot and heel turn with the right foot until they are in the positions indicated at d and f. The right foot crosses at e first and also at x and all the other crossings. This figure does not represent a very pretty movement, because it is made up of straight lines and angles, but it is a good one to learn because it gives proficiency in the heel and toe turns. It bears about the same relation to skating as velocity exercises do to piano-playing.

SPREAD-EAGLES.

Fig. 36. This is a well-known movement in which the performer gains a momentum by any forward movement, the locomotive being one of the best, and placing the heels together and toes in opposite directions and making a long, continuous roll as far as the momentum acquired will carry. The heels should be placed within at least twelve inches of each other, the nearer the better; knees straight. During the performance of this movement, a jump may be made, turning half around or completely so. The Reverse-foot Principle, Fig. 50, is used in all the spread-eagles.

GUIDE FOOT ROLLS.

Fig. 37. This is the same as the plain forward outside roll, Fig. 26, except that the balance foot, which we will now call guide-foot, is allowed to keep the toe on the floor behind the floor foot. That is, each foot connects its flat-foot rolls with a compound curve toe roll, as shown by the dotted lines in Fig. 37.

Fig. 38 is performed backward the same as forward, with the exception of making the toe-guide rolls in front of the floor foot instead of behind.

The guide-foot rolls should be learned both inside

and outside, forward and backward, on heels and on toes. When performed on the heels or toes the figure may be somewhat varied, as shown in Fig. 39, by holding the foot still at b while that part of the stroke ac between the letters e and x is being made. While the left foot is going from x to c, the right foot is going from b to z, and while the right foot is going from z to y the left is held still at c, &c. The Change of Heel and Toe Principle is used in all Guide-foot Rolls.

Fig. 40. This is a Promenade Step which may be performed to 3-4 or 2-4 time. The dotted lines indicate the toe rolls except the short curves, ab and de. At a the right foot is brought down flat while at the same time the left foot makes a toe turn at c by lifting the heel at a and passing it over to b, as indicated by the dotted line ab. These two movements performed simultaneously make the second beat in the measure if the movement is being performed to 2-4 time, but if being performed to 3-4 time, it accents the first beat in each measure. In 2-4 time, the first beat of the next measure is made by the flat-foot roll af and the toe roll cd, the toe roll always coming in behind the flat-foot roll. This movement should also be learned with a heel roll guide.

PIVOT - FOOT ROLLS.

Fig. 41. This is only a practice movement it not being very pretty on account of the wide separation of the feet at times. The right foot is going from c to d while the heel of the left foot is making the turn from a to b; and the left foot goes from b to f while the right is making the turn from d to e. This is using the toe as the pivot. The heel may also be used as a pivot. This movement is used in figure eights. It is also something like the Pivot Reverse-foot Principle, Fig. 6.

THE MERCURY.

The position is the same as in one-foot leading serpentines. The momentum is gained and a long roll made as in the spread-eagles, except the position of the feet is different.

FLYING TURNS.

Fig. 42. The Principle of the Turn is used in this movement. Start forward with Fig. 32 skulling movement. Then after a slight momentum is gained, make a toe turn on both toes turning to the right; then make a heel turn on both heels turning to the right again, and so on. The heel and toe turns as made in this movement are called double heel turns or double toe turns, as the case may be. Practice this movement with the feet close together as possible until it can be performed very rapidly; it is preliminary to the grapevines. The turn on both toes or both heels should be made simultaneously.

Fig. 43 is the same as Fig. 42, except the toe turns are not made simultaneously; neither are the heel turns. The toe turn at c made on the right toe is made just before the toe turn at d made on the left toe; or, in other words, the heel of the right foot is brought from a to b and then the heel of the left foot is brought from b to e. And in like manner the heel turn at h is made before the heel turn at f. The turns so made are called broken turns. This movement should be thoroughly practiced if you desire to learn the grape-vines. The same movement should be learned turning to the left. Figs. 42 and 43 should be practiced and learned thoroughly on the heels, toes, right heel and left toe, and left heel and right toe.

Fig. 44 is the same as Fig. 42, with the exception that instead of simply making a double toe turn, say at c, a heel and toe whirl is made by whirling on the left heel and right toe. The same kind of a whirl is made at e, etc. This movement is called " The Flying Turn with whirl." Remember to practice this movement turning to the left as well as turning to the right. Practice also on heels, toes, right heel and left toe, and left heel and right toe.

FLYING WHIRLS.

Fig. 45. This is performed on the toes with the body constantly turning to the right. The left foot is held at b while the right goes from a to c; and the right foot is held at c while the left goes from b to d; and so on. Never allow the flat-foot to touch in this movement. The roll from a to c is made with the toe pointing to c, while the roll from c to e is made with the heel pointing to e. The roll from b to d is made with the heel-pointing to d, while the roll from d to f is made with the toe pointing to f. Or, in other words, it is like performing Fig. 43 with the lines or strokes kc and df left out, the toe remaining at k and d while the other stroke is being made past it.

Fig. 46 is the same as Fig. 45, except the body turns continuously in the opposite direction. Both of these figures should be practiced on the toes, heels, and heel and toe.

FLYING TURN GRAPEVINES.

Single. Fig. 47. A double toe turn is made as in Fig. 42, but instead of bringing the feet around as shown by the dotted lines *a* and *b*, a double heel turn is made at *c* and *d*. That is, the toe turns are made as in Fig. 42, and, by the use of the Compound-curve principle, the heel turns are made as at *c* and *d*. This movement may also be made with broken toe and heel turns, which are explained in Fig. 43. A whirl may be made in place of the toe and heel turns, as shown in Fig. 49.

Fig. 48. This is the grapevine interlacing. It is generally performed on the toes by experts; and when so performed, it makes a very showy movement. The body faces *xa*, as shown in the figure, and the right foot passes from *x* to *b*, while the left is held at *a*. In going from *b* to *c* the left is crossed over in front of the right while the body is going backward. But at *c* the left passes rapidly ahead of the right and reaches *e* at the same time the right reaches *d*. Then the right passes very rapidly from *d* to *g*, while the left remains at *e*, but at *g* the left catches up with the right and crosses behind it. At *h* the left passes ahead of the right and reaches *k* by the time the right reaches *i*. This movement should be performed rapidly and with short compound curves, so that it will look much more difficult than it really is.

Double. Fig. 50. A toe turn and then a heel turn are made as in Fig. 42, and then a toe turn and then a heel turn are made. Broken turns may be used instead of double turns. This movement may be defined in general as a toe turn and a heel turn to the right, and a toe turn and a heel turn to the left, each alternate turning to the right and left being connected by a compound curve made on each foot. A whirl may be made in place of the toe turns as shown in Fig. 52.

FLYING WHIRL GRAPEVINES.

Single. Fig. 55. This is a combination of the movements represented by Figs. 45 and 46, the alternate turning to the right and to the left being connected by interlacing compound curves. That is, a whirl is made to the right as in Fig. 45, and then a whirl is made to the left as in Fig. 46.

Double. Fig. 56. This is simply making two flying whirls to the left, and then two to the right, etc.

The grapevines on heels or toes are the showiest and prettiest movements performed on skates. They may be started and ended with a split with good effect.

CONTINUOUS ONE-FOOT FIELD MOVEMENTS.

SERPENTINES.

Fig. 57. This is much like the two-foot serpentines. In both cases a simple waved line is described on the floor. The easiest way to perform this movement is by swinging the balance foot behind the floor foot across the line of motion, as shown in the figure. It may be performed with the balance foot swinging in front of the floor foot or resting on the heel of the floor foot or the toe of the floor foot. The principle of the Compound Curve is used in this movement. Learn to perform all the variations of this movement with very long and curving rolls, as it is preliminary to some one-foot eights.

ZIGZAGS.

Fig. 58. This might also be called a one-foot grape-vine, as it is performed very much in the same way. Learn to perform it as much as possible with acute angles and straight lines. It will be found rather difficult.

MERCURIES.

This is simply gaining an impetus by any forward movement and making a long roll on one toe or one heel. To learn this, get pretty well up on the toe until the toe of the shoe almost touches the floor. Move the balance foot backward and forward parallel with the floor foot. This is done to keep the balance, but of course it looks better to keep the balance foot still. This is preliminary to the one-foot serpentines on heels or toes. It also develops the muscles for all toe and heel business.

FLYING THREES.

Fig. 59. Starting on the inside. This is simply made up of alternate heel and toe turns. The balance foot serves to jerk the body around. The broken threes should be learned before this is attempted. This movement should be learned well, however, as some of the one-foot eights are done upon this principle.

Fig. 60 is the same as Fig. 59, except turning in opposite direction.

Fig. 61 is performed on left foot starting on the inside.

LOCOMOTIVES.

Fig. 62. This is something like the one-foot serpentine with the balance foot swinging behind, but instead of in the air, it touches the floor each time it crosses the line of motion. Each alternate stroke of the balance foot is a reverse-foot stroke. When this movement is made rapidly, it is supposed to imitate the noise of a locomotive. This movement may be varied by lifting the leading foot at each stroke of the balance foot as in Fig. 63; or by making a straight line with the leading foot; also by alternating right and left foot as leading foot at the completion of each second or fourth step. Fig. 64 shows the alternation of leading foot at each second step with the lifting of leading foot at each step. Fig. 65 shows the alternation of leading foot at each fourth step without lifting the leading foot at each step. The variations of Fig. 62 all belong to broken two-foot movements, but are given here because better understood in this connection.

GRAPEVINES.

Single. Fig. 66. This is made by using a toe turn of Fig. 59 and heel turn of Fig. 60, connecting them by a compound curve

Fig. 67. This is made by using a heel turn of Fig. 59 and a toe turn of Fig. 60.

Double. Fig. 68. This is performed by making a toe turn and heel turn as in Fig. 59 and then compound curve, after which a toe turn and heel turn is made as in Fig. 60. The compound curves in this are made going forward.

Fig. 69. This is performed by starting backward, first making a heel turn and then a toe turn as in Fig. 59, and then by a compound curve, making a heel turn and toe turn as in Fig. 60. The compound curves in this instance are made going backward.

Fig. 70 explains itself.

BROKEN TWO-FOOT FIELD MOVEMENTS.

PLAIN OUTSIDE ROLL, BACKWARD.

Fig. 72. This is learned by first learning the backward skull, Fig. 31. After Fig. 31 is learned thoroughly on the flat-foot, then practice Fig. 71, which is the same as Fig. 31, except that the heel of one foot is raised while the other makes an outside roll; or, in other words, one foot makes a toe roll while the other makes an outside roll. Learn gradually to make both the toe roll on one foot and the outside roll on the other

long as possible, bearing less weight of the body on the toe roll and more on the outside roll. Remember the toe roll is always an inside roll. A slight push is given with each foot as it changes from outside roll to inside toe roll. There will be a slight change of flat-foot roll in this movement, as will be seen by examining the figure. This change of roll becomes necessary so that the push may be given. The object of the skater, however, should be to learn to make this with as little a change of roll as possible. Practice this movement well, as it is very necessary to fancy skating.

PLAIN INSIDE ROLL, BACKWARD.

Fig. 74. This movement also is learned by first learning the backward skull, Fig. 31, but instead of learning to make an inside toe roll and an outside flat-foot roll, make an outside toe roll and an inside flat-foot roll as represented by Fig. 73, the dotted line representing the toe roll. This and the preceding movement are very essential and preliminary to all fancy skating, and should be learned thoroughly. Remember to hold the body erect, bearing the weight principally on the rear rollers. In performing these rolls, the head should be turned alternately to the right and left at each stroke so that he may avoid collisions, etc. That is, when a stroke is made on the right foot the head is turned to the left, and when a stroke is made on the left foot the head is turned to the right.

CHANGE OF ROLL

Starting on the inside. Fig. 75. This is simply

making a compound curve on each foot. The figure is sufficiently plain

Starting on the outside. Fig. 76.

Starting right foot on the inside and left foot on the outside. Fig. 77.

These changes of roll should be learned well, both forward and backward.

CROSS ROLLS, FORWARD, OUTSIDE.

Lap-foot front. Fig. 78. This movement is learned by first learning the lap-foot circles forward to the right and to the left. It will then be comparatively easy to learn to always lap the balance foot over and across the floor foot. This is a very pretty movement, and should be learned by all.

Lap-foot back. To learn to execute this with a simple outside roll on each foot is very difficult. The lap-foot back is generally made with a change of roll, starting on the inside, which movement constitutes the "On to Richmond Reverse," as shown in Fig. 79.

CROSS ROLLS FORWARD, INSIDE.

Lap-foot front. Fig. 80. This is quite a pretty movement, in which there is a slight change of roll at the end of each stroke. This change of roll, though, should be made as slight as possible.

Lap-foot back. This gives practically the same movement as the "On to Richmond Reverse." Fig. 79.

CROSS ROLLS BACKWARD, OUTSIDE.

Lap-foot front. Fig. 81. This is what is commonly called the "On to Richmond" movement. It gives the performer the appearance of trying to go forward when he is really going backward.

Lap-foot back. Fig. 82. This is the prettiest backward roll performed on skates. It should be practiced thoroughly, as it is used very much in figure skating. The head is gradually turned from side to side at each roll; for example, at the commencement of the right foot roll the head is turned to the left, and at the commencement of the left foot roll the head is turned to the right. The balance foot is carried slowly around to stroke position as represented by the dotted lines. Where the dotted line crosses the floor foot line it represents the balance foot passing behind the floor foot. This roll may be started by first taking standing position with the right foot heel at the hollow of the left foot, and then throwing the weight back in the direction which the heel of the right foot indicates, and at the same time bringing that foot back behind the left, to stroke position. The movement may also be started with a backward skull.

CROSS ROLLS BACKWARD, INSIDE.

Lap-foot front.   Fig. 83.
Lap-foot back.   Fig. 84.

EXTRA PUSH ROLLS.

Forward outside. Fig. 85. This is made by simply giving a push with the balance foot at the beginning of each stroke.

Backward, outside. Fig. 86. This is also made by giving a push with the balance foot at the beginning of each stroke.

If the floor foot is lifted after each extra push the movement then will be the polka step roll No. 2. Fig. 88.

POLKA STEP ROLLS.

Forward, plain. Fig. 87. In this case the roll is broken into three strokes, or it takes three strokes to make one roll. In the figure the first stroke is on the right foot, outside, the second on the left foot, inside, and the third stroke on the right foot, outside. The roll to the left is made by first an outside stroke on the left, second, an inside stroke on the right, and third, an outside stroke on the left. The plain forward and backward, the forward with lap-foot front and backward with lap-foot back may be performed to 3-4, 4-4, or 6-8 time by lengthening the third stroke of each roll to suit. In 4-4 time the third stroke is made long enough to take up the last two beats in the measure; and in 6-8 time the third stroke is performed during the last four beats, counting six beats to the measure. The forward polka step rolls with lap-foot back and the backward with lap-foot front, should be performed to 4-4 time or 6-8 time. No. 176 in the list of movements when performed to 6-8 time, giving three beats to the whirl, is a very pretty and at the same time rather difficult movement

LOCK-FOOT ROLLS.

Fig. 90. The left foot makes lap-foot back at *a* and

then the right is lifted at the end of the stroke at *b* and placed down at *c*, thereby making a reverse-foot step.

Fig. 91.   This is the same as the preceding except that the right foot makes a toe turn at *b*, instead of being lifted entirely off the floor.

Fig. 92.   A slight stroke is made on the left foot from *a* to *b*, while the right foot is being lifted from *c* to *d*; and at *e* a slight toe-turn is made, bringing the heel around as indicated by the dotted line.   This movement is rather difficult; each forward roll is on the inside.

Fig. 93.   This is like the preceding, with the exception that at *e*, instead of turning the body around to the right, the body is turned to the left, and then a compound curve is made on the left foot.

Fig. 94 is performed backward, starting each roll on the inside.   At *a* a lap-foot back is made, and at *b* a cut-off, or reverse-foot, is made, etc.

HALT-FOOT ROLLS.

Plain forward, outside.   This is the plain forward outside roll, with the addition of turning the floor foot up on each toe at the end of every stroke, so that the toe of the shoe will rest on the floor and make a sudden stop.   Plain forward inside is made in the same way.

Forward, outside, lap-foot back.   Fig. 95.   This may be performed to 4-4 time.   The first beat is made by the forward stroke, the second beat is made by the lap-foot back stroke, the third beat is made by turning the floor-foot up on the toe, and the fourth beat is made by bringing the lap-foot around to stroke position. This is used in several figure eights.

Backward outside, with lap-foot front. Fig. 96. This is rather difficult, but should be learned, as the movement is used in several figure eights. The illustration explains itself.

REVERSE - FOOT ROLLS.

Spread-eagle. Fig. 97. This is done by alternating leading foot, making a roll to the outside. The change of leading foot may also be made by a jump, turning half way around. Each spread-eagle roll may also be made to the inside.

Cut-off front, facing left. Fig. 98. This is used in combination with the Dizzy No. 2, reverse-foot. At *a* the cut-off step is made, and at *b* the Dizzy No. 2 step is made.

Cut-off back, facing left. Fig. 99. This is also made in combination with Dizzy No. 2. This and the preceding movement should be practiced well, as they are used in some very pretty figure eights.

Cut-off front, alternating right and left. Fig. 100.

Dizzy No. 1 is used in combination with Dizzy No. 2, making a movement in which the body continuously turns to the right or left. Fig. 101 represents the movement where the body turns continuously to the left, always making a forward stroke on the left foot, and a backward stroke on the right.

The toe-turn reverse-foot may be used in connection with the cut-off back step, making also a movement in which the body turns continuously in one direction. Fig. 102 represents the body turning continuously to the left. A slight toe-turn is made at the end of each left foot stroke.

TOE - WHIRL ROLLS.

This is made by turning to the right or left at the end of each stroke, according to whether the balance foot is swung in front or behind. For example: If the stroke and toe-turn is to be made on the right foot and the balance foot is swung in front, the body will make a turn to the right; but if the balance foot is swung behind, the body will make a turn to the left. It being a complete turn of the body, that is, a turn once around, it is called a toe-whirl to distinguish it from a toe-turn, which is always less than one-half way around. The whirl made by swinging the balance foot back is much easier than the one made by swinging it front. In making balance foot back toe-whirls (Fig. 103) the body should be turned as much to the left as possible before the balance foot swing is made, supposing the balance foot to be the left foot. The fact that the body can be so turned in making a balance foot back-whirl is the reason that this kind of a whirl is easier than the balance foot front-whirls.

HEEL - WHIRL ROLLS.

Fig. 104. That which is said in reference to the toe-whirl rolls applies equally to the heel-whirl rolls. These heel-whirl rolls and the toe-whirl rolls are very showy but rather difficult. They are used in may very pretty figure eights.

FLYING THREES.

Forward, starting on the inside. Fig. 105.

Forward, starting on the outside. Fig. 106.

Backward, starting on the inside. Fig. 107. This necessitates a toe half-whirl at the end of each backward outside stroke. The balance foot is swung back, as indicated by the arrow. This movement is rather difficult but showy. It may be varied by making a cut-off back step. Fig. 108.

Backward, starting on the outside. Fig. 109. This is made with a slight toe-turn at the end of each backward inside stroke, balance foot swung back; or, it may be made with a change of roll and Dizzy No. 1 step. Fig. 110.

All the foregoing flying threes should be learned with a complete toe or heel-whirl at the end of each three.

BROKEN ONE-FOOT FIELD MOVEMENTS.

CHANGES OF ROLL.

The changes of roll on one foot are made with the aid of a hop at the end of each compound curve. They may be performed something like a one-foot serpentine, with a slight hop at every other curve. Fig. 111 shows that the hop is made a little to one side so that a push is given at' *a*, throwing the body into stroke position at *c*. In Fig. 112 the body makes a quarter turn in the air at each hop. All these one-foot changes of roll may be used in the one-foot figure eights.

TOE - WHIRL ROLLS.

These are very difficult but very showy. They are well worth the trouble to learn, as they may be used in one-foot figure eights. A hop is made after each whirl.

FLYING THREES.

These are like the one-foot continuous flying threes, except that they are broken at each turn or alternate turn by a hop or turn in the air. See Figs. 113 and 114.

HOP ROLLS.

The impetus is given by a hop at the end of each stroke, as shown in Fig. 115. They should be learned inside and outside, forward and backward. They are not very pretty, but may be used in one-foot figure eights. They are also preliminary to the one-foot toe or heel rolls.

CHAPTER VIII.

FANCY SINGLE FIGURES. — (CONTINUOUS.)

CIRCLES.

All field movements may be performed in a circle by simply making the line of motion take a circular direction. Of these it is not necessary to speak. There are a few movements, however, which are peculiar to a circular motion, among which are the·lap-foot circles learned in plain single skating. These lap-foot circles should be learned backward as well as forward.

Both the cut-off steps may be used in a circle, either with the face to the center or the back to the center. Fig. 116 represents cut-off front circle with the back to the center, while Fig. 117 represents the same with the face to the center.

There is also a little circle of four strokes, in the performance of which the face is kept constantly in one direction. If the line of motion is to the right, it is performed as follows: First, an outside roll on the right foot; second, by use of the cut-off reverse-foot make a roll backward on the outside of the left foot; third, an inside roll backward on the right foot; and fourth, an inside roll on the left which brings the performer to starting position. See Fig. 118. The same may be performed with the line of motion to the left.

A one-foot circle may be made as shown in Fig. 119, by the use of the hop

The zigzag circles appear complicated to the uninitiated. See Fig. 120.

The flying whirls when performed in a small circle make a very pretty figure. See Fig. 121.

EIGHTS.

Almost all the field movements may be used in a figure eight. It will be apparent from this statement that the list of eights, therefore, will be a large one, and for that reason we will reserve them for a separate chapter.

THREES.

The figure threes are very essential to fancy skating and at the same time rather easy to learn, especially the toe-turn threes. The ideal three is made with a three-quarter circle to each half of the three as represented in Fig. 122; but when it is used in combination with other movements or in field movements, it undergoes many modifications and only retains its character in the toe and heel turns that are made. Beside the heel and toe turn threes, there are the pivot-foot, lock-foot, and cut-off reverse-foot threes, etc.

FIVES.

The figure fives are comparatively easy after the heel and toe turn threes are perfectly learned. They are sufficiently explained in the list of movements and the illustrations.

SQUARES.

This is simply performing some field movement in the general form of a square. The two-foot and one-foot grapevine squares are very pretty. The one-foot grapevine squares may be made with a hop, as in Figs. 128 and 129.

¦HEXAGONS.

This also may be made by performing a field movement in the shape of a hexagon. A one-foot hexagon with hop is represented in Fig. 130

SPLITS.

The splits are defined in a preceding chapter. They are used in starting and ending grapevines, scissors, and eights. A combination of the forward and backward split may be used successfully with a change of heel and toe, making a figure as represented by Fig. 132. The forward and backward split in combination may also be made interlacing, standing still, or moving to the right or to the left, as shown in Figs. 133 and 134, respectively.

Fig. 133 may be performed flat-foot or on toes. When performed flat-foot it is harder for others to discover exactly what the movement is than when performed on the toes. The object is to move the feet from a and c back to b and d, and then to move them forward to a and c again. In moving the feet backward one foot, the right for example, goes a little slower than the left, and crosses in front of it, but reaches b by the time the left reaches d.   In going forward from b and d to a and c, the right foot again goes slower than the left and crosses in behind it, but reaches a by the time the left reaches c.

Fig. 134 is the same movement as Fig. 133, except that the body moves to the right by making each split a little to the right of the preceding split.   For instance, the left foot in being drawn back will go form b to d instead of from b to $a;$ and the right foot will go from f to g instead of from f to e, etc.

SCISSORS.

The prettiest way to perform the scissors is on the toes, although it may be performed flat-foot or on the heels.   They may be performed straight as in Figs. 135 and 136, or interlacing as in Fig. 137.

Fig. 135.   Start at c, let the feet separate and reach d and e, then draw them back to c, where the right foot is brought immediately behind the left, then make a half whirl to the right, going forward in the direction of b with the right foot in advance of the left.   When the split is made at b the feet may be drawn back to f, where another half whirl is made as at first, after which the skater goes back and makes another split at a, etc. The half turn may be made by bringing the left foot immediately behind the right and turning to the left. The rule is if the left foot is behind, turn to the left, and if the right foot is behind, turn to the right.   A whole whirl and a half may be made instead of a half whirl.

Fig. 136 is the same as the preceding, except that the half whirl is made in the middle of the figure instead of at the end.

Fig. 137 may be obtained by simply making Fig. 139 interlacing.

Fig. 138 shows a variation of the scissors which is very pretty. Go from d to a as in Fig. 140, but at a make a three-quarter whirl so that the remaining half of the scissors is made in the direction of c instead of b. From c go back to a and make another three-quarter whirl and go to b; from b come back to a, make a three-quarter whirl and go to e, etc. It may be well here to repeat that all grapevines should be started and ended with a split just as the scissors are started and ended with a split. The object in making the split in these movements is to separate the feet as little as possible, and at the same time give as much impetus to the body as possible by squeezing the feet toward each other as they are drawn back. In making the scissors an additional impetus may be gained in making the half whirl by giving a slight push with the left foot, if the whirl be made to the right, just as the toe points at right angles to the line of motion.

SPINS.

The spins are always very showy, whether performed in connection with other movements or alone. The spin is a prolonged or continued whirl. It should be performed with the arms straight down at the sides, the body erect, and the head up. The length and beauty of the spin depends much upon a perfect balance being maintained. Even a heavy watch will prevent a good spin. During the spin the head should be kept directly over the center of gravity. Spins may be started with pivot-foot circles, splits, flying whirls, or grapevines. When started with flying whirls or grapevines, the body is apt to keep moving onward during the spin. In this case the figure described represents a corkscrew, and for that reason they are known as "corkscrew spins." See Fig. 139.

The one-foot spins are very difficult. They are started with a roll with a sharp curve, a heel turn, and then a spin on the toe as shown in Fig. 140. The balance foot is held in front or behind the other leg. See Fig. 141.

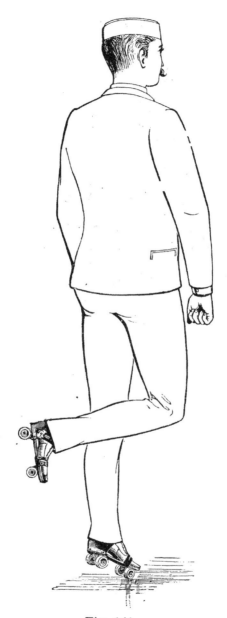

Fig. 141.

CHAPTER IX.

PLAIN COMBINATION.

Combination skating is skating with a partner— lady or gentleman. The plain outside roll is commonly used in this branch of skating, although the inside roll should be learned so that it may be used in the fancy combination. The plain inside roll is not very pretty in either single or combination skating, and it takes considerable practice before it can be performed with anything like grace. When performed as cross roll, however, it is much prettier than the plain roll. The lap-foot circles in combination with a partner, should be learned thoroughly, so that when skating a march, the circle to the right may be performed with a regular stroke, keeping time with the others, and not with a long roll on both feet, until the circle is completed. In a march, the gentleman always starts with the lady on the right; but in general skating, the gentlemen always takes the inside; that is, if the general skating be to the left, the gentleman takes the lady on his right so that he may support her in "turning the corners," but if the general skating be to the right, the gentleman takes the lady on his left for the same reason that he took her on the right in the former case.

The lap-foot circles should be learned with the gentleman on the outside, and also with the gentleman on the inside; that is, the couple should practice lap-foot circle to the left with the lady on the left, and then with the lady on the right; and the lap-foot circle to the right should be practiced with the lady on the left, and then with the lady on the right. It is very necessary that all the circles should be practiced well, so that there will be a unity, or oneness, of motion; because one of the essential points of excellence in combination skating is this uniformity of motion and stroke. The couple should have exactly the same stroke as if governed by one mind, so that in a march, when they separate and skate alone for awhile, they will have their strokes come in exactly right when they again join hands.

Although combination skating is especially enjoyable with an interesting person and a good skater, yet it is in its crudity. Very few of the fancy movements are performed in combination. It is our opinion, however, that in a few years this branch of the art will have advanced so far and so generally throughout the country that skating clubs will be as numerous as dancing clubs. Very many of the simple movements performed singly will become very interesting when performed in combination with a partner.

The proper position for holding the hands and arms in plain combination skating is illustrated in Fig. 142. The lady and gentleman are supposed to be going around the rink to the left. The gentleman takes the

Fig. 142.

lady's right hand in his right hand, and the lady's left in his left, the right arm of the gentleman passing under the lady's left arm.

FANCY COMBINATION.

This is the highest and most difficult branch of the whole art of skating, and the most interesting and enjoyable as well; but, as before remarked, it is yet in its crudity. There are so many beautiful combination movements which can only be performed by experienced skaters, that it is difficult to assemble sufficient talent at any one rink to practice and develop this branch of the art. For this reason we are very much in favor of skating clubs, because they offer time and opportunity for improvement in this particular direction. We sometimes wonder why some ladies and gentlemen do not become tired of skating around the rink in one direction all evening without ever varying their stroke when there are so many pretty combination movements to learn. The combination eight performed by good skaters, where every stroke is precision, affords a pleasure which dancing never can. There are many simple movements, however, which are performed more easily with a partner than without, such as the cross-rolls, the polka steps, the "On to Richmond," etc.

Besides the position of holding, or joining, the hands as given in Plain Combination, and which we will call Position 1, there are several other positions which are graceful and quite easy. We give them below so numbered that they may be conveniently referred to hereafter:

Position 2.   Gentleman on the left; passes his right arm under the lady's left, taking her left hand in his right.   Fig. 142½.

Position 3.   Gentleman to the left; assume Position 2, and then bring the arms straight down to the side, keeping the hands joined and skating close to each other.

Position 4.   Gentleman to the left; takes lady's left hand in his right, but is separated somewhat from the lady.

Position 5.   Gentleman to the right; takes lady's right hand in his right, as in position 1, but instead of joining left hands in front the lady passes her left hand behind her back and joins the gentleman's left, as shown in Fig. 143.

Position 6.   Gentleman behind lady; lady reaches both her hands back with her right hand in his right and her left hand in his left.

Position 7.   Gentleman in front skating backward; takes lady's right hand in his left and her left hand in his right.

Position 8.   Same as Position 7, except the lady skates backward and the gentleman forward.

LONG ROLL ALTERNATING SIDES.

The lady and gentleman assume Position 5, standing with the heel of the right foot at the hollow of the left.   Take one stroke on the right foot.   This gives

Fig. 142½.

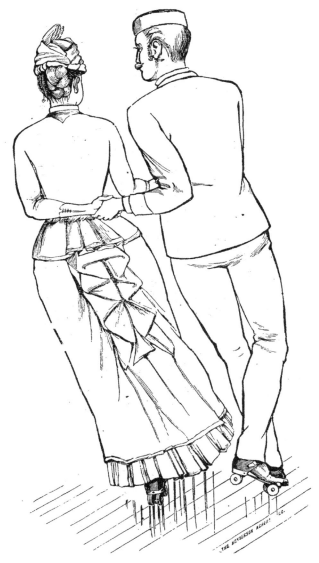

Fig. 143.

sufficient momentum to take a long roll on the left foot. During the long roll on the left foot, the gentleman passes behind the lady and to the other side by curving his stroke more than the lady's stroke. This brings the gentleman on the left side of the lady, with the lady's right hand now behind her back. The next stroke is a long roll on the right foot, during which the gentleman again passes behind the lady and takes his place at her right as at first. Fig. 144 represents the strokes as taken in this movement, the dotted lines representing the lady's movement. This is a very pretty combination movement, and should be learned by everybody, as it may be performed in a simple figure eight or combination eight.

THE MARCH.

The march is one of the prettiest performances on skates. It may be made intricate or not, according to the ability of those who take part. The participants should keep step with each other, every one taking a stroke on the right foot at the same time and of the same length, and then on the left foot at the same time and of the same length. A piece of music in 3-4 time is the best for a simple march; but where the performers are capable, a potpourri is splendid, the performers changing their step at each change of time in the music. A plain polka step will be used to a slow waltz, or a lap-foot back may be used to a piece in 4-4 time or 6-8 time. The promenade step may be performed to waltz time or march time. When a march is varied, not only with all these different steps, but with the various positions of joining hands, it becomes very interesting to the skaters and very pretty to the audience.   The success of the march depends very much upon the lead couple, as they must know their figures thoroughly, and be able as well as the others to execute them nicely.   Each couple should keep about six feet distant from the forward couple.

We give below only a few of the almost endless variety of march movements and figures ·

Fig. 145.   This is what is called a plain march figure eight.   The skaters follow the lead couple around in the direction indicated by the arrows.   The ·rectangle represents the boundary of the rink floor.

Fig. 146.   This is performed by each couple separating at *a*, the ladies going to the right as indicated by the light line, and the gentlemen going to the left. Each couple are to join hands again at *b*.

Fig. 147.   This is the same as the preceding figure, except that at *b* the partners are not to join hands, but the gentlemen pass behind their respective partners, as indicated by the heavy line.   The ladies cut the end of the eight opposite from the end which they first cut, and then when ladies and gentlemen come around to *b* they join hands.

Fig. 148.   Partners separate at *a*, the ladies turning to the right and the gentlemen to the left.   At *b* the gentlemen pass behind their respective partners in the direction indicated by the heavy line, and meet their partners at *c*, but passing on to the outside until they come around to b again, where they join hands with partners.

Fig. 149. Disjoin hands at a, the ladies turning to the right and the gentlemen to the left. At b the gentlemen fall in behind their respective partners. Ladies and gentlemen then all go single file until they reach c, where the gentlemen go to the right and ladies to the left, coming around to d, where they join hands again.

Fig. 150. Disjoin hands at a, ladies turning to the right and gentlemen to the left. At b the gentlemen pass to the outside of the ladies, as indicated by Arrow 4, while the ladies go on around to c, as indicated by Arrow 1. At c the gentlemen pass again to the outside of the ladies, going on around, as indicated by Arrow 3, while the ladies go on around towards b, as indicated by Arrow 2. At d the gentlemen pass behind their respective partners, coming around on the middle line in the direction indicated by Arrow 7, while the ladies come around on the outside line in the direction of Arrow 5. At e the ladies pass to the outside in the direction of Arrow 6, while the gentlemen pass to the inside, as indicated by the inside line and Arrow 8. At b the ladies pass again to the outside, as indicated by the middle line, and in the direction of Arrow 5, while the gentlemen come around on the middle line in the direction of Arrow 7. Ladies and gentlemen meet at f and join hands

Fig. 151. Disengage hands at a, ladies turning to the right and gentlemen to the left. At b the gentlemen pass on the inside of the ladies, going around towards *e*, as indicated by Arrow 2, while the ladies go towards *f*, as indicated by Arrow 7. The gentlemen come on around in the direction of Arrow 1, and the ladies in the direction of Arrow 8. The gentlemen meet the ladies at *b*, and pass on in the direction of Arrow 6, while the ladies go around towards *e*, as indicated by Arrow 3. The ladies come on around in the direction of Arrow 4, and meet and pass the gentlemen at *b*. The gentlemen come around in the direction of Arrow 6, while the ladies come around as indicated by Arrow 5. Ladies and gentlemen turn in at *f*, towards *c*, and join hands at *c*.

Fig. 152. Ladies and gentlemen separate at *a*, ladies turning to the right and gentlemen to the left. The gentlemen pass behind their respective partners at *b*, but instead of going in the direction of Arrow 7, they go in the direction of Arrow 4; and the ladies, instead of going in the direction of Arrow 5, go in the direction of Arrow 3. The gentlemen pass behind their respective partners again at *c*, and take the same direction again with which they started out, as indicated by Arrow 1, while the ladies also take the same direction with which they started out, as indicated by Arrow 2. The gentlemen again pass behind their respective partners at *d*, taking the direction of Arrow 5, while the ladies take the direction of Arrow 6. The gentlemen again pass behind their respective partners at *b*, coming around again in the direction of Arrow 7, and the ladies in the direction of Arrow 8. Ladies and gentlemen then turn in and join hands at *e*.

Fig. 153. Let the capital letters represent the gentlemen and the small letters represent the ladies. Then let a pass in front of A around to F, as indicated, and at the same time let A pass behind a around to f. Then in the same manner let b pass around to E, and B pass around to e. And then in the same manner c · goes around to D and C around to d, and so on. Then it will be found there are two rows of couples with the ladies on the left. Then let the first couple in the row on the right fall in behind the first couple in the row on the left, and the second couple on the right fall in behind the second couple on the left, and so on, until there is only one row, as represented in Fig. 154. Then c passes in front of D around to C, and at the same time D passes behind c to d; and while the first two couples are thus exchanging for their original partners, the second and third couples are also exchanging in the same manner. Then Aa lead off, Ff falling in behind Aa and Ee behind Bb, etc.

Fig. 155. Ladies and gentlemen form a circle with hands disjoined. The ladies stand still while the gentlemen pass in and out among the ladies as represented by the waved line in the illustration. The dots represent the ladies. When the gentlemen come around to their original position, they stand still, while the ladies skate in and out among them in the opposite direction from which the gentlemen skated. When the ladies come around to their original position, they do not stop, but continue in the same manner while the gentlemen again pass in and out as they did at first.

This last is very much like the " Grand right and left " in a quadrille ; and right here we will state that many of the dance figures may be performed very pleasingly on skates.　When the lead couple meet again they leave the circle and start off on some other figure and the other couple follow.

The object of the lead couple should be to make the march as varied as the ability of the participants will allow.　This may be done by varying the step and stroke, by varying the manner of taking partners' hands as given in the eight positions, and by varying the figures.　Where the size of the rink will admit, the long roll alternating sides in a plain forward movement is very fascinating to the participants and beautiful to the spectators.

It is not necessary to give any further movements or figures to be performed in a march, as the lead couple with a little ingenuity may arrange them without end.

THE MAY-POLE.

This is a very pretty performance, and always attracts a large audience.　As many different colored ribbons are fastened at the top of the pole as there are skaters who take part in twining them about the pole. Fig. 160 is the figure movement used in the twining of the ribbons.　The twining of the ribbons should be preceded by a march of indefinite length.

THE MASQUERADE.

When properly conducted, the masquerade is very interesting to all.　Masquers should all be required to raise their masques at the door, so that all objectionable characters may be excluded. If a certain clique wish to masque and skate with only members of the clique without knowing their identity, an emblem of membership may be chosen beforehand, such as a blue ribbon on the right arm, etc.

Besides the foregoing, there are many other amusing performances on skates, such as the potato race, where each contestant is required to take from a row of potatoes one at a time and put them in a basket at the other end of the room. Then there is a tournament where the contestants are provided with long poles with which they take rings suspended about four feet above their heads. Foot-ball on rollers creates much amusement.

THE FIGURE EIGHTS.

The figure eights are all obtained from field movements, as will be readily perceived by the following examples.

Fig. 156 shows how it is obtained from the plain forward roll, and also how it should be practiced. Gradually learn to curve each roll more and more until a complete circle is performed on either foot readily. This, then, is the plain forward eight on the outside. It is learned on the inside in the same manner, curving each stroke more and more until a complete, or rather in this particular case not quite complete circle is made on either foot.

Fig. 157 shows how the eight is obtained from the serpentine roll, either on two feet or one foot.

Fig. 158 shows how it is obtained from flying turns.

Fig. 159 shows how it is obtained from flying whirls.

With these few examples we think the reader will understand how to perform a figure eight obtained from almost any and every field movement. This is the secret of the many pretty figure eights which professional experts perform. It will be observed that by following out this principle of manufacturing or inventing the figure eights that there is almost no limit to the variations of this figure.

Fig. 160 is the plain outside forward.

Fig. 161 is the plain inside forward.

Fig. 162 is the two-foot serpentine, left foot leading.

Fig. 163 is the two-foot serpentine, right foot leading on one circle and left leading on the other circle.

Fig. 164 is the guide-foot eight, outside

Fig. 165 is the pivot-foot eight, inside.

Fig. 166 is the flying turn eight.

Fig. 167 is the flying turn grapevine eight.

Fig. 168 is the flying whirl eight.

Fig. 169 is the one-foot change of roll eight, continuous.

Fig. 170 is the flying three on right foot and then on left foot.

Fig. 171 is the plain outside backward eight.

Fig. 172 is the plain inside backward eight.

Fig. 173 is the change of roll on right foot to be followed by change of roll on left foot.

Fig. 174 is the cross roll eight, forward.

Fig. 175 is the cross roll eight, backward.

Fig. 176 is the change of roll eight, starting on the inside of each foot.

Fig. 177 is the halt-foot eight with lap-foot back.

Fig. 178 is the reverse-foot at *a* and lap-foot front at *b*.

Fig. 179 is the toe whirl eight with balance foot swung back as indicated by the dotted lines.

Fig. 180 is the one-foot change of roll eight, with hop.

Fig. 181 is the one-foot change of roll eight, with two hops.

Fig. 182 is the one-foot dumb-bell eight.

Fig. 183 is the one-foot dumb-bell eight, with one hop.

Fig. 184 is the one-foot dumb-bell eight, with two hops.

THE COMBINATION EIGHTS.

These are the prettiest of all combination movements, and require more precision and ability than is usually found in most skaters, especially ladies.

The plain forward outside roll is performed as a figure eight, as illustrated in Fig. 185. The gentleman cuts a small circle while the lady cuts the large one, and the lady cuts the small circle while the gentleman cuts the smaller one. The light lines represent the lady's strokes.

Fig. 186. This is obtained from the long roll alternating sides. The light lines represent the lady's strokes. It may be performed with the lady on the outside or inside.

Fig. 187.   This is performed without joining hands at all.   The gentleman, whom we will call A, and the lady, whom we wil¹ call B, take a standing position, as indicated at *a* and *b*.   A cuts circle 1 on the right foot while B cuts circle 2 on the right foot.   At *x* each passes to the left of the other.   Then A cuts circle 2 on the left foot and B cuts circle 1 on the left foot, and then at *x* they pass to the right of each other, etc.

Fig. 188.   Let A cut circle 1 while B cuts circle 3, both on the right foot, in the direction of Arrows 1 and 2, respectively.   Then let A cut circle 2 on the left foot in the direction of Arrow 3, and B cut the same circle on the left foot, as indicated by Arrow 4.   Then A cuts circle 1 again while B cuts circle 3 again, etc.   While A and B are cutting circle 2 they may join left hands until the circle is completed.

Fig. 189.   Let A and B cut circles 1 and 3 as in Fig. 188, and let C and D cut circles 4 and 5 while A and B are cutting circles 1 and 3, all on the right foot. Then let A and B cut circle 2, during which they join left hands, and at the same time C and D cut circle 2, joining hands in like manner.   Then A and B and C and D cut circles 1, 3, 4, and 5 simultaneously, as at first, etc.   This may be varied by having A and B cut circles 1 and 3 while C and D are cutting circle 2, and then A and B cut circle 2 while C and D cut circles 4 and 5, etc.

Let A cut circle 1 and B cut circle 3, as in Fig.

188, and then proceed to circle 2, as in Fig. 188, also, but instead of A going back to circle 1 and B to circle 3, A goes only to circle 5 and B to circle 4. A and B then cut circles 4 and 5 in the same manner as they cut circles 1 and 3. Then after cutting circle 2 again, A goes to circle 3 and B to circle 1, and so on until A comes back to circle 1 and B comes back to circle 3. This figure may be performed by four persons.

Fig. 190. Let A and B cut circles 1 and 3 as in Fig. 188, and C and D cut circles 3 and 4 in like manner, while E and F cut circles 3 and 6, and G and H cut circles 3 and 9, also in like manner. Then let A and B cut circle 2 with left hands joined, while C and D cut circle 4 also with left hands joined, and E and F cut circle 7, and G· and H circle 8 at the same time and in the same manner. Then each skater cuts his or her original circle as at first.

THE EXPERT'S EXHIBITION.

There are now a great many amateur as well as professional exhibition skaters, while several years ago they were only to be seen in the larger cities. A few suggestions to those who are just starting out may not be amiss:

1. Proceed from the simpler figures to the more difficult ones

2. Have your movements programmed and committed to memory.

3.   Do not try to give all the variations of any one general figure or theme.

4.   Figures with a whirl or spin are generally more showy than many more difficult figures which have only a plain movement.

5.   Never repeat a movement in the same exhibition.

6.   Do not try some movement only half learned.

7.   Don't always think you are the best skater present and act accordingly.

The exhibition skater may introduce many novel features, according to his fancy and proficiency, such as cutting the figure eights with a chair in each circle, or perform the interlacing serpentine with wine glasses in a row as indicated by the dots in Fig. 191, etc. Skating on stilts is quite a difficult feat, and always takes well. The hand-spring is another good performance; also skating with the skates entirely unfastened.

LIST OF MOVEMENTS.

The following list comprises most all the movements known to professional skaters. Those in *Italic* type are explained and illustrated in the preceding chapter, while the others will be readily understood from previous explanations of principles and variations, and from the connection they have to those in *Italic* type. Flatfoot is understood, except where otherwise stated.

PLAIN SINGLE.

Plain forward outside roll. Fig. 26.
Plain forward inside roll. Fig. 28
Lap-foot circle to the left. Fig. 29
Lap-foot circle to the right. Fig. 30.

FANCY SINGLE.

CONTINUOUS TWO-FOOT FIELD MOVEMENTS.

SKULLS.

1. *Forward.* Fig. 31.
2. " Fig. 32.
3. .. Fig. 33.
4. *Backward.* Fig. 31.
5. .. Fig. 32.
6. '' Fig. 33.
7. Nos. 1, 3, 4, and 6, on heels.
8. " " " " " " on toes.
9. " " " " " " on right heel and left toe.
10. " " " " " " on left heel and right toe.

SERPENTINE.

11. *Forward, right foot leading.* Fig. 34.
12. " left " "
13. Backward, right foot leading.
14. " left " "
15. Nos. 11, 12, 13, and 14 on heels.
16. " " " " " " on toes.
17. " " " " " " on rt. heel and lft. toe.
18. " " " " " " on lft. heel and rt. toe.

ZIGZAGS.

19. *To the right.*   Fig. 35.
20.   left.

SPREAD-EAGLES.

21. *Straight, right foot leading.*   Fig. 36.
22. Inside, right foot leading.
23. Outside, "   "
24. Straight, left "
25. Inside,   "   "
26. Outside,   "   "
27. Nos. 21, 22, 23, 24, 25, and 26 on heels
28.   "   "   "   "·   "   "   "· " on toes.
29.   "   "   "   "   "   "   "   " on r. h. and l. t.
30.   "   "   "   "   "   "   "   " on l. h. and r. t.
31. Nos. 21 to 30, inclusive, with serpentine movement.

GUIDE-FOOT ROLLS.

32. *Forward, with toe-guide.*   Fig. 37.
33. *Backward, "*   Fig. 38.
34. Forward, with heel-guide.   Fig. 37.
35. Backward, "   Fig. 38.
36. Nos. 32, 33, 34, and 35 on toes.
37.   "   "   "   "   "   " on heels.
38.   "   "   "   "   "   " on r. heel and l. toe.
39.   "   "   "   "   "   " on l. heel and r. toe.
40. Nos. 32 and 39, inclusive, inside and outside.
41. *Promenade step, forward, with toe-guide.* Fig. 40.
42.   ..   "   "   " heel-guide.

43. Promenade step, backward, with toe-guide.
44.   "   "   heel-guide.
45. Nos. 41, 42, 43, and 44 on toes.
46.   "   "   "   "   "   " on heels.

PIVOT-FOOT ROLLS.

47. *Forward, inside, with toe-pivot.* Fig. 41.
48. Backward,   "   "
49. Forward,   "   "   heel-pivot.
50. Backward,   "   "
51. Forward, outside, with toe-pivot.
52. Backward,   "   "

MERCURIES.

53. *Forward, right foot leading, on toes.*
54.   "   left   "   "
55.   right "   "   on heels.
56.   left   "
57.   right '   on r. h. and l. t.
58.   right   on l. h. and r. t.
59.   left   "   "   on r. h. and l. t.
60.   left   "   "   on l. h. and r. t.
61. All Mercuries backward.

FLYING TURNS.

62. *Turning to the right.* Fig. 42.
63.   "   "   *left.*

FLYING WHIRLS.

64. *Turning to the right on toes.* Fig. 45.
65.   "   "   *left*   "   Fig. 46.

66. Turning to the right on heels.
67.   "   "   left
68.   "   "   right on right heel and left toe.
69.   right on left heel and right toe.
70.   "   left on right heel and left toe.
71.   "   left on left heel and right toe.

FLYING TURN GRAPEVINES.

 72. *Single, facing right.* Fig 47
73.   "   "   "   *interlacing.* Fig. 48.
74.   "   "   left.
75.   "   "   interlacing.
76. *Double with compound curve, forward.* Fig. 50.
77.   "   "   "   "   *backward.*   "
78. *Double.* Fig. 53.
79. All flying turn grapevines on toes.
80.   "   "   on heels.
81.   "   "   "   r. heel and l. toe.
82.   "   "   "   l. heel and r. toe.
83. All flying turn grapevines with interlacing compound curves.
84. All flying turn grapevines with whirls.

FLYING WHIRL GRAPEVINES.

85. *Single on toes, interlacing.* Fig. 55.
86. *Double, "   "*   Fig. 56.
87. Single, on heels, "
88. Double, on heels, "
89. Single, on right heel and left toe.
90.   "   on left heel and right toe.
91. Double on right heel and left toe.
92.   "   on left heel and right toe.

ONE-FOOT CONTINUOUS FIELD MOVEMENTS.

SERPENTINES.

93. *Right foot forward,* balance foot swinging in front. Fig. 57.

94. *Right foot forward,* balance foot swinging back. Fig. 57.

95. *Right foot forward,* balance foot resting on toe.

96. " " " " " " on heel.

97. Left foot forward, balance ft. swinging in front.

98. " " " " " " back.

99. " " resting on toe.

100. " " " " " " heel.

101. Right foot backw'd, bal. foot swinging in front.

102. " " " " " " back.

103. " " " " " resting on toe.

104. " " " " " " " heel.

105. Left foot backward bal. foot swinging in front

106. " " " " back.

107. " " " " " resting on toe.

108. " " " " " " heel.

109. Nos. 94, 98, 102 and 106 on toes.

110. " " " " " " " heels.

ZIGZAGS.

111. *Right foot to the right.* Fig. 58.

112. " " " left.

113. Left foot to the right.

114. " " " left.

FLYING THREES.

115. *Right foot, starting forward on the inside.*
Fig. 59.

116. *Right foot, starting forward on the outside.*
Fig. 60.

117. Left foot, starting forward on the inside.
Fig. 61.

118. Left foot, starting forward on the outside.

LOCOMOTIVES.

119. *Right foot leading, continuous.* Fig. 62.

120.   "   "   "   *broken.* Fig 63.

121. Left foot leading, continuous.

122.   "   "   "   broken.

123. *Alternating right and left at each fourth step.*
Fig. 64.

124. All Locomotives backward. Fig. 65.

125. Alternating forward and backward. Fig. 66,

126. Nos. 119 to 125, inclusive, on toes.

127.   "   "   "   "   "   " heels.

128.   "   "   "   "   "   " r. heel and l. toe.

129.   "   "   "   "   " l. "   " r. "

GRAPEVINES.

130. *Single, facing right.* Fig. 67.

131.   " left. Fig. 68.

132. *Double, with two turns, compound curve forward.* Fig. 69.

133. *Double, with two turns, compound curve backward.* Fig. 69.

134. *Double, with three turns.* Fig. 70.

BROKEN TWO-FOOT FIELD MOVEMENTS.

135. *Plain outside roll, backward.*   Fig. 72.
136.   " *inside* "   Fig. 74.

CHANGES OF ROLL.

137. *Forward, starting on the inside.*   Fig. 75.
138. Backward,   "   "   "   "
139. Forward, starting on the outside.   Fig. 76.
140. Backward,   "   "   "   "
141. Forward,   "   right foot inside, left foot outside.   Fig. 77.
142. Backward, starting right foot inside left foot outside.
143. Forward, starting left foot inside, right foot outside.
144. Backward, starting left foot inside, right foot outside.
145. All changes of roll with toe whirl.
146.   "   "   "   "   heel   "
147.   "   "   "   lap-foot front.
148.   "   "   "   "   "   back.
149.   "   "   "   halt-foot.
150.   extra push.
151.   "   "   "   "   "   polka step.

CROSS ROLLS.

152. *Forward, outside, lap-foot front.*   Fig. 78.
153.   "   *back.*
154.   *inside*   "   *front.*   Fig. 80.
155.   "   *back.*   Fig. 79.

156. *Backward, outside lap-foot front.*   Fig. 81.
157.   "   *back.*   Fig. 82.
158.   *inside*   "   *front.*   Fig. 83.
159.   "   "   "   *back.*   Fig. 84.
160. All cross rolls with extra push.
161. "   "   "   "   polka step.
162. "   "   "   "   halt foot.

EXTRA PUSH ROLLS.

163. *Forward, outside.*   Fig. 85.
164.   "   *inside.*
165. *Backward, outside.*   'Fig. 86.
166.   "   *inside.*

POLKA STEP ROLLS.

167. *Forward, plain.*   Fig. 87.
168. Backward, plain.
169. *Forward, with lap-foot front, No. 1.*   Fig. 88.
170.   "   "   " 2.   Fig. 89.
171.   "   "   "   "   " 3.
172.   "   "   back,   " 1.
173.   "   "   "   "   2.
174.   "   " 3.
175. Nos. 169 to 174, inclusive, backward.
176. *Forward with toe whirl, balance foot front.*
177.   "   "   "   "   back.
178.   " heel whirl   "   " front.
179. "   "   "   "   " back.
180. Nos. 176, 177, 178, and 179 backward.
181. *Forward, with halt-foot on second beat.*
182.   "   "   " third

183. Backward, with halt-foot on second beat.
184.   " third "
185. Forward, with reverse-foot on second beat.
186.   " " " third   "
187. Backward, with reverse-foot on second beat.
188. All polka step rolls on the inside.

HALT-FOOT ROLLS.

189. *Plain forward, outside.*
190.   "   "   " with extra push.
191.   "   "   " *with lap-ft. back.* Fig. 90.
192.   "   *inside.*
193.   "   with extra push.
194. "   " lap-foot back.
195. *Backward, outside, lap-foot front.*

REVERSE-FOOT ROLLS.

196. *Spread Eagle with outside roll.* Fig. 97.
197. "   " " inside roll.
198. *Cut-off front, facing left.* Fig. 98.
199. "   " " right.
200.   *back* " *left.* Fig. 99.
201. "   " " right.
202. *Cut-off front, alternating rt. and lft.* Fig. 100.
203. " back,   right and left.
204. *The Dizzy, turning to the left.* Fig. 101.
205. "   "   right.
206. *The Toe-turn Reverse-foot, turning to the left.* Fig. 102.
207. The Toe-turn Reverse-foot, turning to the right
208. *Pivot Reverse-foot, turning to the left.*

209. Pivot reverse-foot, turning to the right.

210. Nos. 204, 205, 206 and 207 alternating right and left.

211. Nos. 202, 203, and 210 with toe whirls.

212. " " " " " " heel whirls.

213. Nos. 198, 199, 200, 201, 202 and 203 with polka step, facing right.

214. Nos. 198, 199, 200, 201, 202 and 203 with polka step, facing left.

215. Nos. 198, 199, 200, 201, 202 and 203 with polka step, alternating right and left.

216. Nos. 202, 203, 210 and 215 with toe whirls at end of alternating stroke.

217. Nos. 202, 203, 210 and 215 with heel whirls at end of alternating stroke.

218. Nos. 202, 203, 210 and 215 with halt-foot whirls at end of alternating stroke.

219. Nos. 202, 203, 210 and 215 with lap-foot whirls at end of alternating stroke.

TOE WHIRL ROLLS.

220. *Forward outside, balance foot back.* Fig. 103.

221.   " " front.

222.   inside " " back.

223. "   " " front.

224. Backward outside, balance foot back.

225.   " " front.

226.   inside,   " back.

227.   " " front.

HEEL WHIRL ROLLS.

228. Same variations as toe whirl rolls. Fig. 104.

FLYING THREES.

229. *Forward, starting inside.*　Fig. 105.
230. 　　　　　　" 　outside.　Fig. 106.
231. *Backward, starting inside.*　Fig. 107.
232. 　　··　　　　··　　Fig. 108.
233. 　　　　　　　outside.　Fig. 109.
234. 　　" 　　　　　Fig. 110.
235. With toe or heel whirls at end of each three.

BROKEN ONE-FOOT FIELD MOVEMENTS.

CHANGES OF ROLL

236. *Forward, starting inside.*　Fig. 111.
237. 　　　　　　outside.
238. 　　　　　　*alternately.*
239. Backward, starting inside.
240. 　　　　　　" 　outside.
241. 　　" 　　　　alternating.
242. Nos. 236, 237, and 238' with toe turn.
243. Nos. 239, 240, and 241, with heel turn.
244. Nos. 239, 240, and 241, with toe whirls.
245. Nos. 236, 237, and 238, with heel whirls.
246. Nos. 236 to 245, inclusive, on the other foot.

TOE WHIRL ROLLS.

247. Forward outside.
248. 　　　　inside.

FLYING THREES.

249. *Starting forward inside on right foot.*　Fig. 113.
250. 　　　　" 　　　" 　　" 　　" 　　" 　Fig. 114.

251. Starting forward inside on left foot.
252.   outside on *right* foot.
253.   "   " left foot.

HOP ROLLS.

254. *Forward outside.* Fig. 115.
255.   inside.
256. Backward, outside.
257.   "   inside.

FANCY SINGLE FIGURES.

CIRCLES

258. *Lap-foot forward, to the right.* Fig. 30.
259.   "   "   ' *left.* Fig. 29.
260.   "   backward to the right.
261.   "   "   " left.
262. *Cut-off front, to the right, with face to the cen-*
ter. Fig. 116.
263. *Cut-off front, to the right, with back to the center.*
264.   "   "   " left,   " face   "   "
265.   "   "   "   "   " back   "   "
266. Cut-off back, to the right, with face to the
center.
267. Cut-off back, to the right, with back to the
center.
268. Cut-off back, to the left, with face to the center.
269.   "   "   "   "   " back   "   "
270. *Facing one way to the right.* Fig. 118.
271.   " left.
272. *One foot circle to the right, outside, forward.*
Fig. 119.

273. One foot circle to the right, inside, forward.

274.   "   "   outside, backward.

275.   "   inside,

276.   "   left, outside, forward.

277.   "   "   "   inside

278.   "   "   "   outside, backward.

279.   "   "   "   inside,

280. All one foot circles with the other foot.

281. *Zigzag circle to the right, back to center.* Fig. 120.

282. Zigzag circle to the left, back to center.

283.   "   right, face to   "

284.   "   "   left,

285. *Flying whirl circle to the right.* Fig. 121.

286.   "   "   "   " left.

THREES.

287. *Right foot starting forward on the outside.* Fig. 122.

288. Right foot starting forward on the inside.

289. Left   "   "   outside.

290.   "   "   "   "   inside.

291. Right foot starting backward on the outside.

292.   "   "   inside.

293. Left   "   "   "   outside.

294.   "   "   "   inside.

295. *Pivot-foot threes starting on left foot inside.* Fig. 123.

296. Pivot-foot threes, starting on right foot inside.

297. Pivot-foot threes, backward.

298. *Lock-foot threes, starting on right foot outside.*
Fig. 124.

299. Lock-foot threes, starting on left foot outside.

300. Lock-foot threes, backward.

301. *Cut-off threes, reverse foot front, starting right foot outside.* Fig. 125.

302. Cut-off threes, reverse foot front, starting left foot outside.

303. Cut-off threes, reverse foot back, starting right foot outside.

304. Cut-off threes, reverse foot back, starting left foot outside.

FIVES.

305. *Right foot, starting forward inside.*
306. "   "   "   *outside.*
307.   "   backward inside.
308. "   "   "   "   outside.
309. Left   forward inside.
310. "   "   "   outside
311.   "   backward inside.
312. "   "   "   outside.

SQUARES.

313. *Continuous two-foot.* Fig. 131.
314.   "   one-foot.
315. *Broken one-foot.* Fig. 129.
316.   "   "   Fig. 128.

HEXAGONS.

317. *Broken one-foot, on right foot.* Fig. 130.
318.   "   " left "

319. Continuous, right foot.
320.   "   left   "

SPLITS.

321. Forward on flat foot.
322. Backward on flat foot.
323. Forward on toes.
324. Backward on toes.
325. Forward on heels.
326. Backward on heels.
327. Forward on right heel and left toe.
328.   "   " left "   " right toe.
329. Backward on right heel and left toe.
330.   " left "   " right toe.
331. Forward and backward, combined, to make interlacing. Fig. 134.
332. Forward and backward, combined, to make interlacing. Fig. 135.

SCISSORS.

333. *Straight, with half-whirl at one end.* Fig. 135.
334.   "   "   " *in middle.* Fig. 136.
335. *Interlacing.* Fig. 137.
336. *Variation.* Fig. 138.
337. Nos. 332, 333, 334, 335, on flat foot.
338. "   "   "   "   " toes.
339. "   "   "   "   " heels.
340. "   "   "   " " r. heel and l. toe.
341. "   "   "   "   " l. heel and r. toe.

SPINS.

342.   Both heels to the right.
343.   "   "   "   left.
344.   "   toes   right.
345.   "   "   "   left.
346.   Right heel and left toe to the right.
347.   "   "   "   "   "   "   left.
348.   Left heel and right toe to the right.
349.   "   "   "   "   "   "   left.
350.   Right toe to the right.
351.   "   "   "   left.
352.   " heel   "   right.
353.   "   "   "   left.
354.   Left toe to the right.   Fig. 141.
355.   "   "   "   left.
356.   " heel   right.
357.   "   "   "   left.
358.   Nos. 341 to 348, inclusive, performed as cork-screw.   Fig. 139.

FIGURES OF ·MOVEMENTS.

Following this are the Figures of Movements described in this work from pages 32 to 85, inclusive.

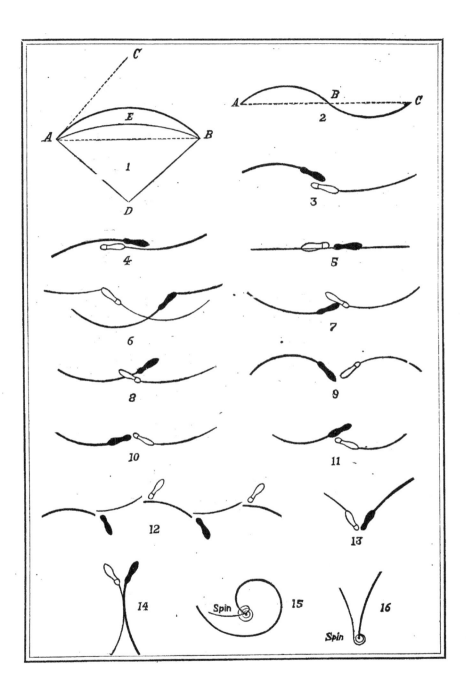

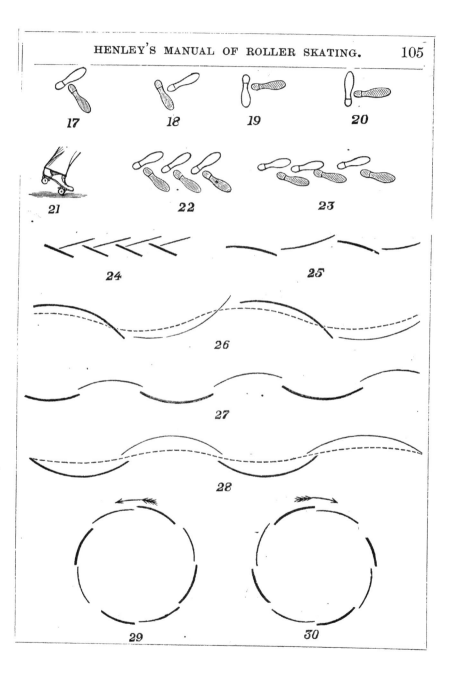

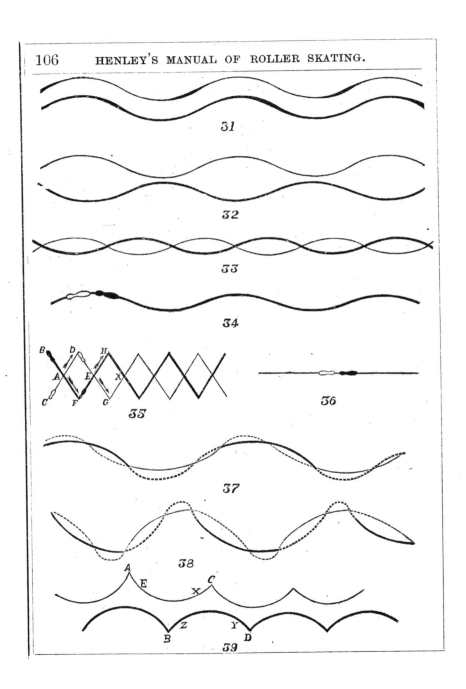

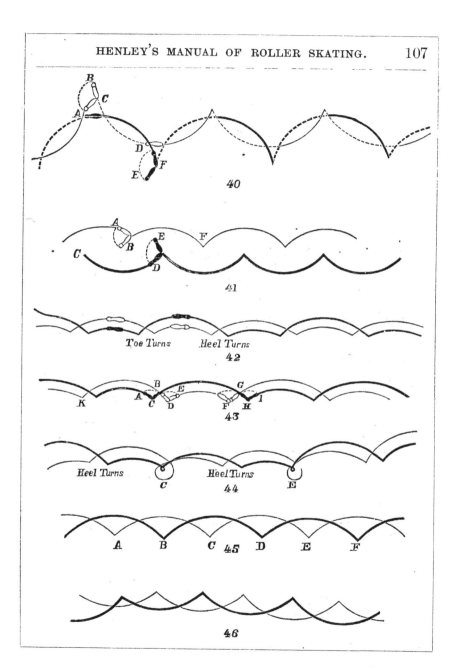

40

41

Toe Turns   Heel Turns
42

43

Heel Turns   Heel Turns
44

A   B   C 45 D   E   F

46

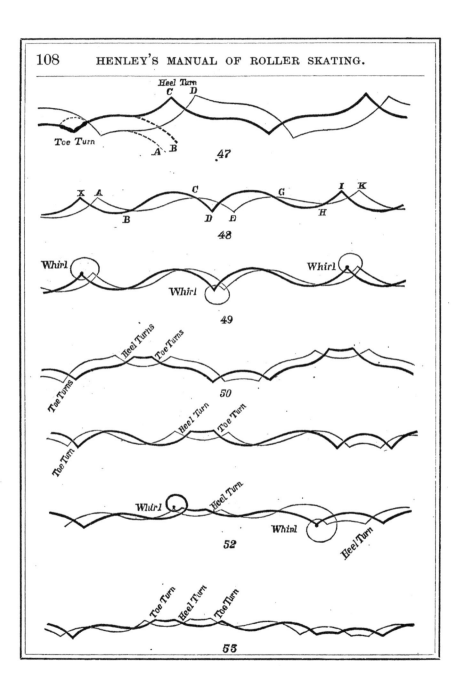

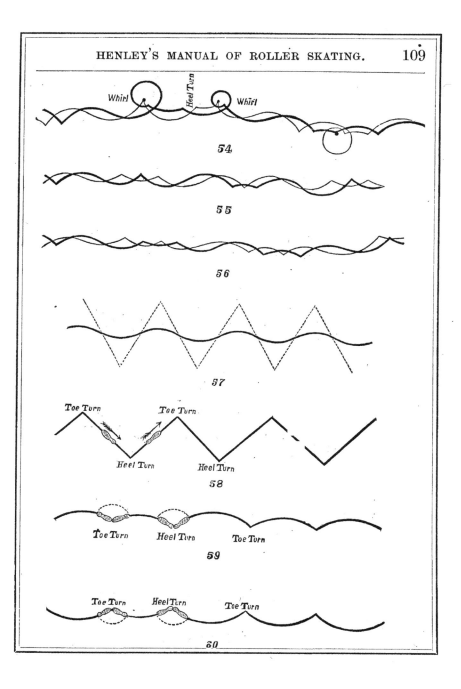

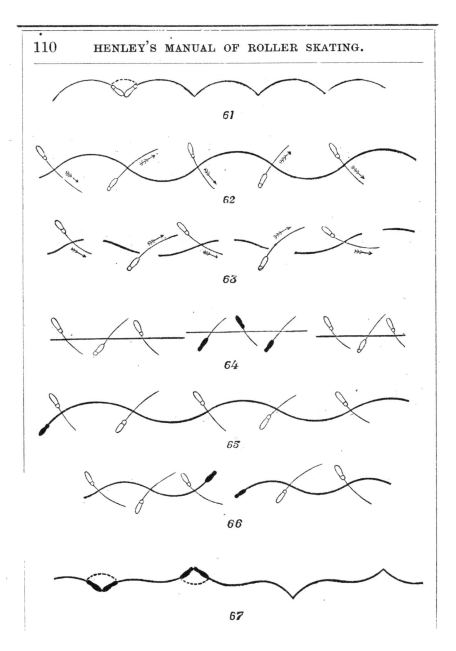

61

62

63

64

65

66

67

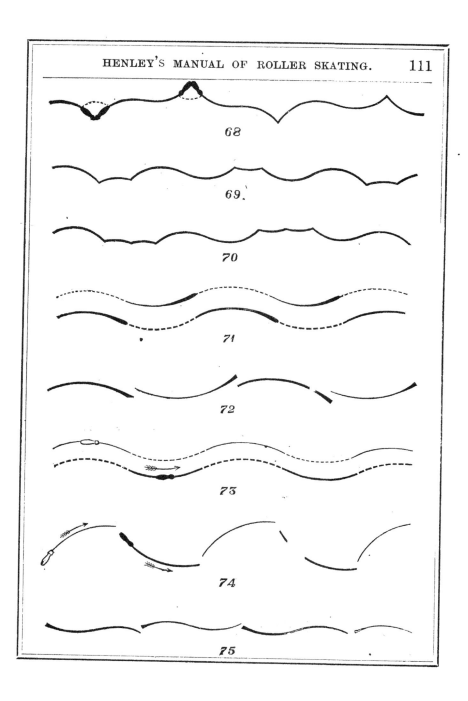

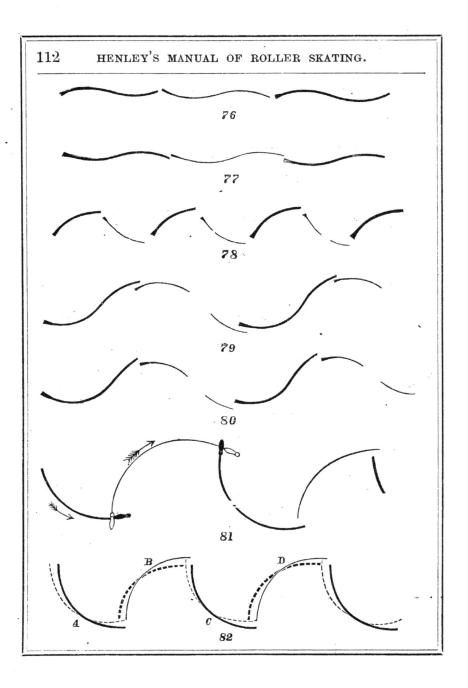

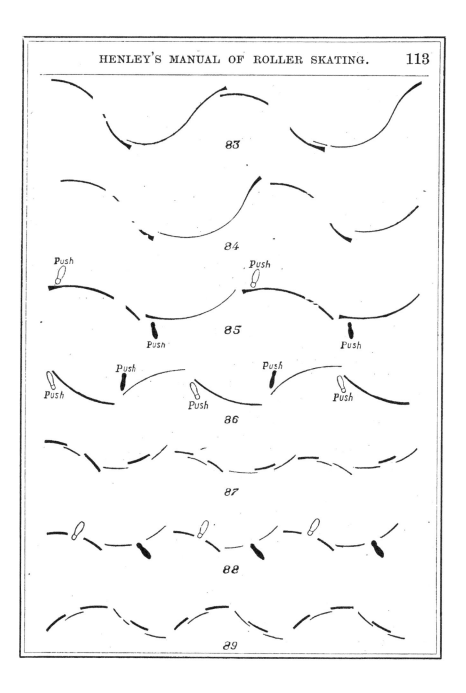

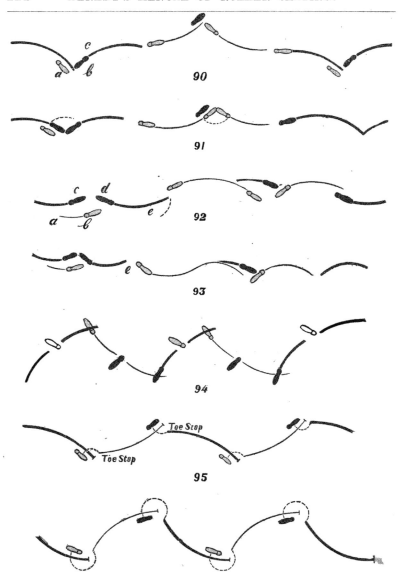

90

91

92

93

94

95

97

98

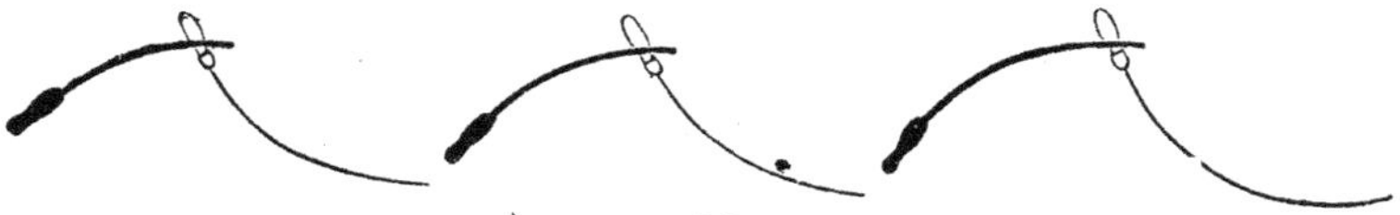

99

100

101

102

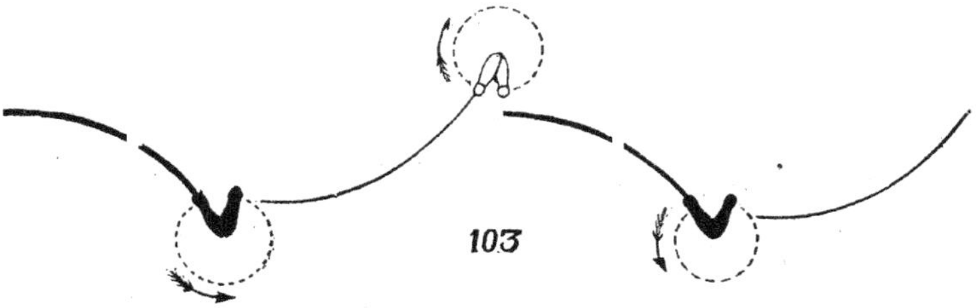

103

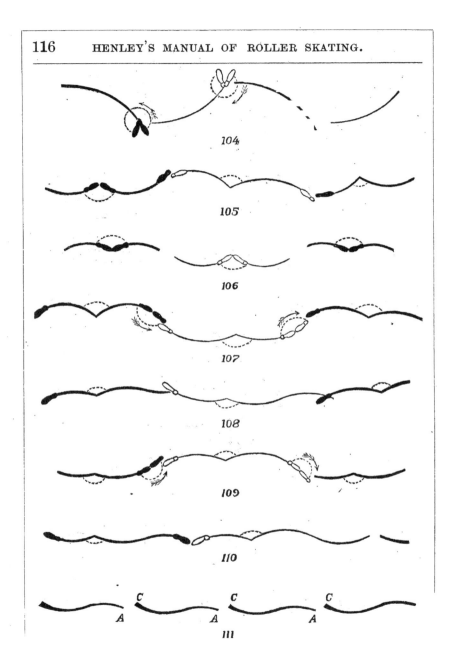

104

105

106

107

108

109

110

111

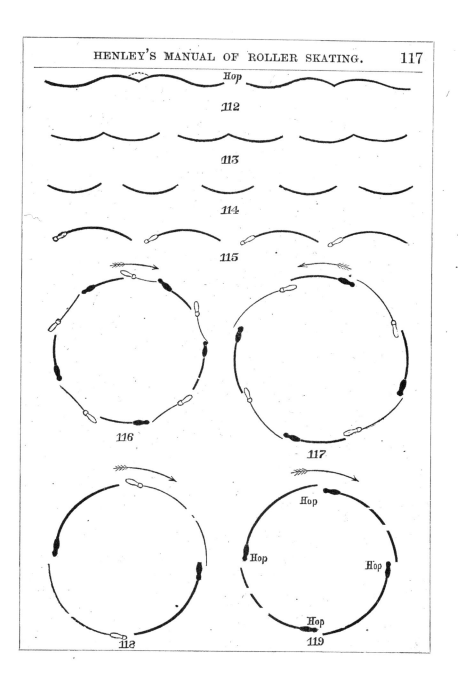

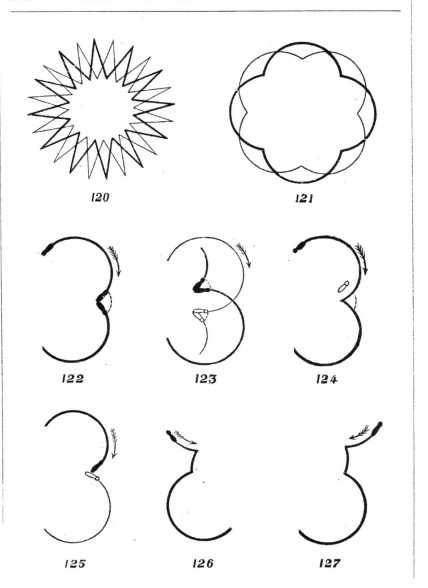

120

121

122

123

124

125

126

127

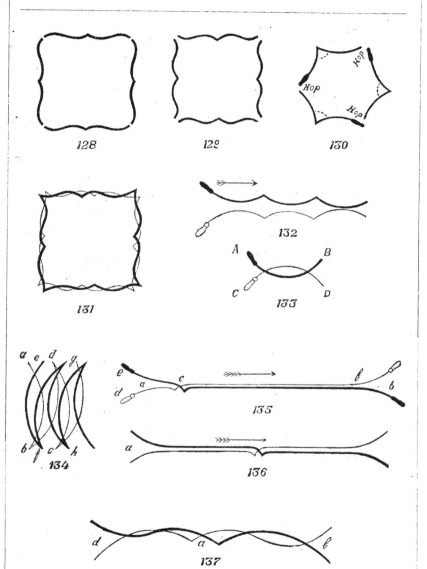

128   129   130

131

132

133

134   135

136

137

138

139

140

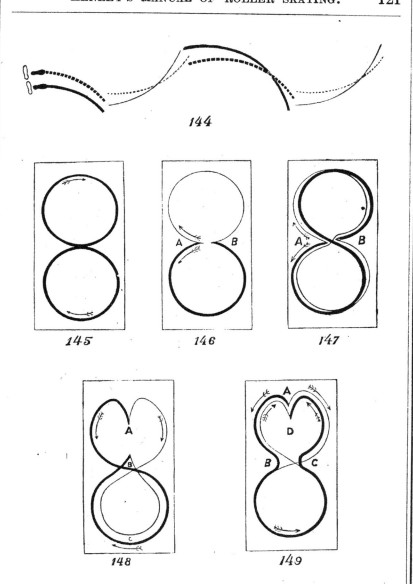

144

145   *146*   *147*

148   *149*

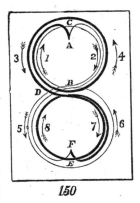

150

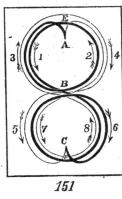

151

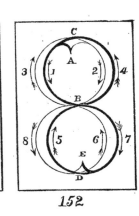

152

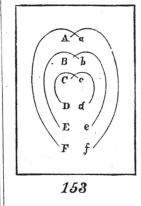

153

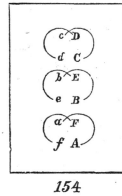

154

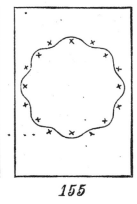

155

156

157

158

159

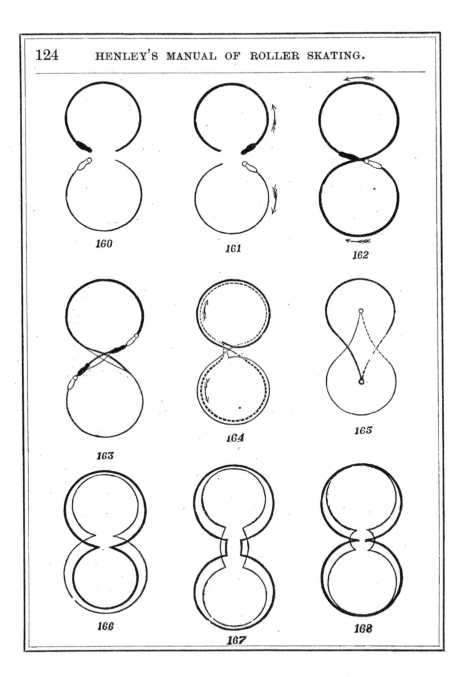

160

161

162

163

164

165

166

167

168

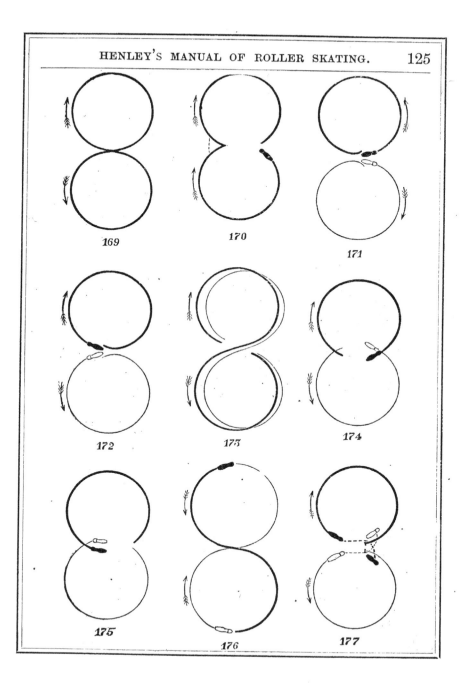

169

170

171

172

173

174

175

176

177

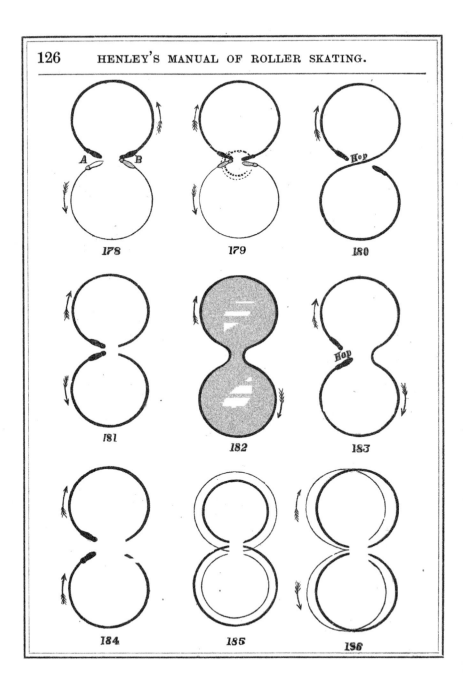

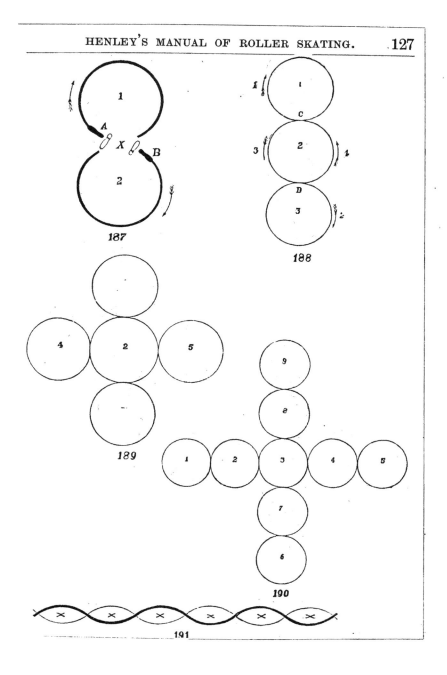

187

188

189

190

191

CHAPTER X.

A PROMINENT PASTOR'S OPINION OF ROLLER SKATING.

As a people we are far behind our English cousins in our love for manly physical sports, and our American stock is so degenerating that many of our girls cannot skate a mile without contracting various disorders. Instead of denouncing the roller rinks, I take pleasure in stating that I consider them a means of grace. I skate myself, enjoy it heartily, and only regret my lack of leisure which prevents my devoting more time to this exhilarating pastime. In my judgment a minister can find no better preparation for his Sunday work than to take his wife and children to the rink on Saturday night and skate about with the young people of his congregation until half past nine o'clock. It will clarify his mind, make him elastic, and put him in good bodily trim for the Sabbath. Moreover, it will give him a good sweat, which latter is an excellent thing for the clergy. My diagnosis as touching the average minister is that he eats too much, and does not take sufficient exercise. Consequently he is inclined to regard the world from the standpoint of a dyspeptic, and not as a red-blooded, vigorous Anglo-Saxon. Some ministers complain that the rinks have affected their audiences for the worse. They have not diminished my audiences in the least. Contrariwise, they were never so large as at present. My opinion is that any church which condemns so morally harmless and physically beneficent an amusement as roller skating, is doing its best to alienate the young people and beget in them a dislike for churches in general. If our churches would secure the sympathies and affections of the young, they must put away all prudery, and take a hearty interest in all forms of innocent and healthful diversion. There are some amusements upon which the devil has not as yet placed his poisonous fingers, and roller skating is one of them. It is far better for church people to patronize this form of amusement, and maintain it in its present innocence and purity, than to turn the cold shoulder upon it and give it over wholly into the hands of Satan. Rightly does the church frown upon such pleasures as are vicious and corrupting, but why this wholesome, refined, and æsthetic amusement should meet with ministerial disapprobation is beyond my power of comprehension.—Rév. JOHN L. SCUDDER, pastor of the First Congregational Church, Minneapolis.

AN EMINENT PHYSICIAN'S OPINION.

In a letter on the subject from one of the most eminent physicians of this country, he says: Nothing has ever taken with our best citizens as roller skating has done, and nothing ever set on foot for the amusement and physical improvement of young people is more worthy of encouragement. Roller skating is just the thing wanted by our young people, especially the ladies. It affords just the sort of exercise they require for their physical development — gentle, but active, and so attractive they can not resist it. It is my deliberate opinion that no conception has ever entered the human mind, in this century, so important to the health of ladies in our cities as this skating within doors. Nothing could exceed it in grace. No sight I have ever beheld is so beautiful as a roller skating rink, with its tastefully dressed young men and ladies sailing, swimming, floating through the mazes of the march, as if impelled by magic power. The old people assemble nightly to witness the sight, apparently as much delighted as their children. All honor, I say, to the inventor of roller skates. Long may he live. The children will rise up and bless his name.

WHAT BISHOP McTYEIR SAYS:

Allow me to commend to you and your readers the Roller Skating. It can — it should — substitute dancing as an exercise and amusement for the young people of both sexes. It furnishes in-door graceful, lively exercise, both muscular and nervous excitement, and leaves no excuse for dancing. I wish there was a skating rink in every village and boarding school. — *Letter to Christian Advocate, April 7th, 1870.*

ROLLER SKATING AND MENTAL HEALTH.

BY DR. T. L. BROWN, OF BINGHAMTON, N. Y.

[Read at Forty-Second Anniversary American Institute of Homœopathy, June, 1885.]

Observation and comparison, with a view to correctly determine the good and evil upon all classes, compel me to decide in favor of roller skating for those who, by their increased mental work, are deprived of the necessary muscular exercise. It is a prescription a physician can take himself without fearing to soon share the same fate of his drugged patient, who needed exercise more than medicine. I have been summering and wintering on roller skates. I have been on the wheels two hundred and fifty times. I have seen fifty-five years of life—thirty years in practicing medicine before putting on the rollers. When I first saw young people roller skating I thought it seemed so easy. When I put them on, I soon discovered that I had not met with anything which could take the conceit out of me as fast as the easy-moving wheels. It took twenty evenings to learn to balance one hundred and ninety-six pounds in a manner so that those who observed me were not as often raising their faces with uncontrollable laughter. From that day to this I have been steadily gaining physical and mental control by this regular exercise.

I last weighed two hundred and two pounds, mostly mere muscle, and correspondingly less carbon tissue. I took the exercise for health and amusement combined. I have never seen a year of as good nutrition and sound sleep as the past year, under the influence of roller skating. It is not a craze to the person who utilizes it for social amusement and health. People who have not tested the exercise are not wise on the subject. Whatever they say about it needs more correction and criticism than skating. We should skate as we eat, sleep, or tell the truth, just for the utility and the improvement it will individually produce. The fittest men and women are daily doing this for the good and happiness it gives them and others. Temperance and exercise furnish evidence of individual mental health in those who practice both. Skating unites the body and mind more intimately than walking or running, with less fatigue for a similar amount of effort.

RULES AND REGULATIONS FOR ROLLER SKATING RINKS.

1. Skating begins with one stroke of the gong, and ceases at two strokes of the gong.

2. No smoking allowed in or about the premises.

3. Gentlemen will not soil the floor with tobacco, and others will not be permitted to do so.

4. Crowding, loud talking, or other rude or noisy demonstrations are forbidden.

5. In putting on skates, see that the buckles are upon the outside of the foot.

6. No one should stand, even for a moment, upon the floor, within skating limits, or so as to obstruct the entrance to the surface or the view of others.

7. Never cross the floor in passing to or from a seat; always follow the direction of the skaters.

8. Spitting, or throwing any substance whatever upon the floor is dangerous, and will not be permitted.

9. Going up or down stairs with skates on is dangerous, and is strictly prohibited.

10. No cane, stick, string, or other similar article should be taken upon the floor.

11. In skating around the circuit all will observe a uniform direction, taking great care never to interfere with the movements of others.

12. No skater should stop, even for an instant, in the circuit, except to assist a lady.

13. Pushing, tripping, racing, tagging, or taking hold of other's garments, or any dangerous actions, are strictly forbidden.

14. Most falls occur from the feet being parallel with each other, or nearly so, as in this position one foot cannot check the movement of the other; hence, before attempting to stand upon the skates, the beginner should place the heels together, with the feet at right angles in which position they should *always be while getting up, sitting down, or standing upon skates.*

15. Skating by four, or more than two together,

should be avoided, while skating in couples should be practiced as much as possible by all sufficiently advanced, as there is no way in which a lady and gentleman can make so graceful and attractive an appearance.

16.   On removing the skates, return them to the skate room, with the heel strap of one skate buckled and tucked firmly into the buckle of the other skate, to prevent mismating.

17.   A cheerful compliance with the above, and a careful regard for the comfort and enjoyment of others, is respectfully requested.

18.   None but those known, or supposed by the management to be acceptable to a majority of the patrons, can be admitted and furnished with skates.

CHAPTER XI.

THE CELEBRATED HENLEY ROLLER SKATES.

From the "Manufacturers' Record."

The past year has been a very eventful one in the history of Roller Skating. This attractive, healthful, and innocent recreation has taken such a firm and permanent hold on the American people that it is now fully recognized and established as the great National amusement.

The demand for good Roller Skates has been enormous, and far in excess of the supply thus far. This unprecedented demand has induced many persons to embark in their manufacture, and has resulted in throwing on the market a large number of cheap and worthless skates—most of them being poor imitations of the better class of goods, and consequently dealers, and most rink owners, have confined themselves to the purchase of skates made by the leading and older manufacturers, of which M. C. HENLEY, of Richmond, Ind., stands preeminently foremost as the most widely-known and largest manufacturer in the world.

We have heretofore noted in our columns that Mr. Henley has contributed more to the advancement of Roller Skating than all others by introducing to the public the celebrated MONARCH AND CHALLENGE ROLLER SKATES, the most durable and complete skates ever put on the market. Not less than one million pairs of the HENLEY SKATES are in actual use in the various leading rinks of this and other countries, and the continued and rapidly increasing demand for them attests their popularity and superiority.

The elegant new factory building, erected by Mr. HENLEY last year, has proved totally inadequate for the trade, and he has been compelled to build a very large addition — making a brick building, in the aggregate, 50x250 feet, four stories in height, slate roofed, with a fine 75-horse power engine, and completely fitted with an immense amount of new and most approved machinery. It has a capacity of turning out 2,000 pairs of Rink Skates, and 500 pairs of Club Skates per day, and giving employment to 300 skilled and efficient workmen.

A detailed description of the various kinds and styles of skates and skate goods manufactured at this famous establishment need not be given here, as their value, elegance of design and workmanship, durability, and general utility are too well known and acknowledged to require any commendation at our hands. Suffice it to say, that the HENLEY SKATE leads the trade, and has been adopted on its merits, and is in general use in most of the Rinks everywhere. It is quite a safe assertion that there are more of the HENLEY Skates in practical and successful use to-day than all others combined.

Mr. HENLEY is constantly making valuable additions and improvements on his skates and patents, and he will doubtless not only keep the manufacture of his goods up to their present high standard, but will, also, if it is possible to do so, increase their efficiency and good qualities. He has recently perfected and placed on the market the new style skate, known as the "MONARCH," having an encased rubber cushion, which has been received with great favor. He is also making an elegant expert skate for fancy and acrobatic skating, and racing. The HENLEY Sidewalk Skate has also been placed on the market, and is a superior skate of the kind.

In concluding this very limited notice of the HENLEY SKATE, we wish to congratulate Mr. HENLEY on his great success in the past, and wish him continued and increased prosperity.

SEND 25 CENTS

----- FOR -----

HENLEY'S OFFICIAL

POLO GUIDE

Playing Rules of Western Polo Leagues,

AND NEW YORK, NEW ENGLAND, AND MASSACHUSETTS POLO LEAGUES,

WITH FULL

INFORMATION AND INSTRUCTIONS FOR PLAYING POLO.

PUBLISHED BY

M. C. HENLEY,

NOS. 523 TO 533 NORTH SIXTEENTH ST.,
RICHMOND, IND.

POINTS OF SUPERIORITY OF THE

HENLEY

Monarch Roller Skate

OVER ALL OTHERS.

By the use of rubber springs the requisite tilting or lateral motion is secured, and the skate is easily changed to suit a heavy or light person, and the skate will turn a two-foot circle, and all the wheels rest square on the floor.

The rubber springs being completely boxed, are absolutely free from oil and dirt, and fully protected from wear.

The truck and frame can be instantly removed by simply drawing back the coupling pin, which is held in position by a strong wire spring, and the rubber springs can be adjusted or replaced in a moment.

By the use of a tension screw the skate is easily adapted to persons of heavy or light weight.

The boxwood wheels are provided with metal boxes, making the skate very light running and durable. It is admirably adapted to amateur and fancy skating, as the tension of the rubber springs can be graduated to suit any skater.

It is symmetrical in its proportions, elegant in its style, of superior workmanship, strong and durable, and is

THE MONARCH ROLLER SKATE OF THE WORLD.

THE IMPROVED

Henley Challenge Roller Skate.

OVER 500,000 PAIRS

NOW IN USE.

This Light Running, Adjustable, Improved Roller
Skate is Offered to the Public on Its
Established Merit.

→ The Success of the Past, a Guarantee of the Future. ←

POINTS OF SUPERIORITY

—OF THE—

Henley Challenge Skate

OVER ALL OTHERS.

By the use of rubber springs the requisite tilting or lateral motion is secured, and the skate is easily changed to suit a heavy or light person, and the largest skate will turn a two-foot circle, and all the wheels rest square on the floor.

The truck and frame can be instantly removed by simply drawing back the coupling pin, which is held in position by a strong wire spring, and the rubber spring can be adjusted or replaced in a moment. The **BOXWOOD WHEELS** are provided with **METAL BOXES**, making the skate very light running and durable. It is admirably adapted to amateur and fancy skating, as the tension of the rubber spring can be graduated to suit any skater.

It is symmetrical in its proportions, elegant in its style, of superior workmanship, strong and durable, and is

The Challenge Roller Skate of the World.

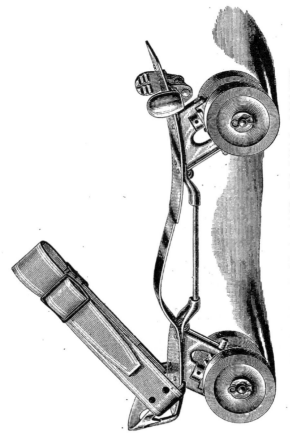

HENLEY'S POLO AND RACING SKATE.

HENLEY S

Polo and Racing Skate.

THE LATEST AND BEST.

THIS light running and durable Skate combines all of the advantages of the celebrated Monarch and Challenge Roller Skates, and is especially adapted and intended for Polo Playing and Speed Skating. By the addition of the stiffening rod the spring steel foot-board is strengthened to meet the demands of Polo, Speed, and Acrobatic Skaters, yet retaining a desirable elacticity, making the skate soft and easy to the foot. Fitted with roll-bearing wheels, the speediest skate in the market is secured, and this skate is offered to the public as the most complete and perfect Polo and Racing Skate ever manufactured, combining greater points of beauty, finish, style, and durability than all others, and is sure to meet that favor and approval its merits deserve.

HENLEY

POLO GOODS.

No. 2.

$1.00 Each.

No. 3.

No. 4.

HENLEY

Regulation Goal Posts.

$5.00 per Set

of Four Posts.

HENLEY

Regulation Stick.

50 cts. each.

COMPLETE UNIFORMS

FOR POLO CLUBS.

WORSTED,

Consisting of Jersey, with one letter on breast; Knee Tights, plain colors; Cap, with or without stripe; Stockings, fine quality.

PRICE, PER UNIFORM, $10.00.

FLANNEL

Consisting of Shirt, with one letter on breast; Pants, Cap, Stockings, Double Buckle Belt.

PRICE, PER UNIFORM, $9.00.

WHEN ORDERING SUITS

Please give full instructions in regard to measurements, colors, etc.

Extra Fine Polo Caps; Fine Blue Cloth, with Gold Cord over top; each, $1.00.

Reasons Why

THE

HENLEY ⚜ ROLLER ⚜ SKATES

ARE THE BEST.

FIRST.

Because— They are easy-running, light, neat, and durable.

SECOND.

Because — They are made of the best material, are elegant in their proportions, and superior in style.

THIRD.

Because — By use of the pressure plate, they are easily adapted to persons of heavy or light weight.

FOURTH.

Because — Their wheels of Turkish boxwood, with Babbitt metal boxes, are far more durable and light-running, while every part is admirably in proportion, combining strength, durability, and symmetry.

FIFTH.

Because — They have been universally adopted when used in competition with any other style of skate, and stand unrivalled, and occupy the proud position of the MONARCH AND CHALLENGE ROLLER SKATES OF THE WORLD!

Endorsement of Prof. Fletcher.

$\mathcal{G}$N a recent letter, containing an order for a pair of Skates each for himself and wife, for use on the stage, Professor FLETCHER, who is acknowledged to be the best and most accomplished Roller Skater in the world and whose wonderful, graceful, and phenomenal performances on Roller Skates have astonished and delighted vast audiences in Europe and America, says of the HENLEY SKATE:

"After having tried, I believe, every style and kind of Skate worthy of attention in this country and England, I freely pronounce the Henley Skate to be far superior to them all, and will use no other hereafter. It is lighter running, quicker in movement, and in every respect better than any other. You have my unqualified and hearty endorsement for your valuable Skate, and I am under obligations to you for furnishing me with what I have been seeking, namely: a perfect, graceful, and scientific Skate, not only eminently fitted for finest performances on the stage, but also for all practical skating, and especially for use in public halls and Roller Skating Rinks."

how to Order Goods.

Terms, net cash on delivery of goods.   Freight or Express charges always to be paid by the purchaser.

☞ All goods sent C. O. D., unless the order is accompanied by P. O. Order, or Draft.   When goods are to be sent C. O. D., one-third the amount must accompany the order.

☞ **Always give name of Express Company you wish goods shipped by.**

The Adams and United States are the only companies having offices in this city.   These offices receive goods for all other Express Companies.

Goods may also be sent by Freight, if desired, when the order is accompanied by one-third the amount.   A draft for the balance will be attached to the bill of lading and sent to bank for collection, and upon payment of same the bill of lading will be delivered to the purchaser.

It often occurs that goods shipped by freight are delayed in transit. To prevent such delays it is always best to ship by Express.

SPECIAL NOTICE.

☞ I request that all parties ordering sundries, parts, repairs, etc., will send **CASH IN ADVANCE,** to prevent any delay caused by sending invoice.   In making remittances always send P. O. Order, Ex. M. Order, or Draft.   No checks will be accepted.

☞ No order amounting to less than **TEN DOLLARS** will be filled unless accompanied by a remittance for the full amount.   I do not wish to open any small accounts, as it causes such an amount of unnecessary and expensive detail.   If too much money should be sent, the balance will be returned.

The Seven Ages of the Roller Skater.

All the world's a rink,
And all the men and women merely skaters ;
They have their exits and their entrances ;
And one man in his time plays many parts,
His acts being seven stages :   At first the ragged
Urchin, rolling 'round the sidewalk on one skate
The terror of all the passers by.   Then the
Beginner, led around the maple with
Awkward steps and sudden plunges, perspiratio
Streaming from his every pore, a sight to look upon.
And then the callow youth, with cap on head
Bearing the word "Instructor," in gilt letters,
Whose duty 'tis, as he considers it, to skate
With all the pretty girls, and leave the struggling
Learners to themselves.   Then comes the fancy skater,
The Professor, who travels all the country 'round
To fill engagements ; a tremendous hero —
In his own estimation.   And then the fair
Young damsel, who glides around the floor as if
It was her native element and roller
Skating her usual mode of locomotion.
Then the mature matron, with gold eye-glasses,
Rolling around with stately dignity,
Gazing with calm placidity upon
The giddy throng.   Last stage of all, that
Ends this short nonsensicality, is
Pater familias, or erst the "Governor,"
Who comes to bring the children,
But, having been enticed to put on skates,
Still comes, and comes, and comes again,
And seems to like it.   W. K.

HENLEY'S MONARCH FENCE MACHINE.—Patented.

HENLEY'S

PATENTED.

PERFECTION ATTAINED AT LAST

In a Fence Machine that any man or boy
can use, and make more and better
fence in one day than with any
other two machines in
the world.

I do not claim to have the only machine for weaving the wire and picket fence, as there are other machines in use which make the fence in strips or rolls of about 50 feet, and these are stretched from post to post and nailed up.   The expense of such machines is beyond the reach of the average farmer, and beside this they cannot make a fence that will in any way compare with the fence made by the MONARCH machine.   There are other machines which attempt to make a fence somewhat similar to the MONARCH, but they have proven worthless and are flat failures as compared with the MONARCH, as will be fully shown by the following

COMMON SENSE REASONS WHY

THE

Henley Monarch Fence Machine

Is the Best and Has No Equal.

BECAUSE the wire is stretched the full length of the field before the weaving is commenced.

2.   BECAUSE any sized wire can be used, and with this advantage: using a large size wire, the strongest fence can be made.

3.   BECAUSE any size, length, or style of picket, or slat or board, can be used, weaving all equally firm and solid.

4.   BECAUSE the picket or slat can be woven in more firmly and solidly than in any other machine.

5. BECAUSE it will make a fence over rough and un-even ground, or up and down hill alike, making as good a fence as on even, level ground.

6. BECAUSE the MONARCH machine stretches the wire tighter, thus making the strongest and best wire and picket fence.

7. BECAUSE any one can operate it, and there are no parts to get out of order or repair.

8. BECAUSE a boy can work it as well as a man, it being light and easily managed.

9. BECAUSE it is made of the very best materials, and, with proper care, will last a life-time.

10. BECAUSE the price is within the reach of every farmer.

11. BECAUSE it is the only machine that forces the slat or picket firmly against the wire, thus securing the slat in such a solid and permanent manner that it can not be pulled out, and breakage is impossible.

12. BECAUSE the fence made by this machine will turn all kinds of stock, and is much stronger than any barb wire fence, and completely obviates all danger of injury to stock; and finally,

BECAUSE it makes the handsomest, best, strongest, and most durable fence, and is the only first-class, practical Fence Machine in the world.

The foregoing are only a few of the points of superiority of the MONARCH FENCE MACHINE over all others, and a trial will convince any one of its merits, and that it has no equal.

THE HENLEY MONARCH FENCE MACHINE

Will weave a handsome picket fence for lawns, gardens, and fronts of lots, and, with great rapidity and regularity, will make the most substantial fence for farms and stock ranches. The MONARCH machine is making a complete revolution in the methods of fencing. The fence made by this machine is destined to rapidly supersede all other styles and kinds of fence, both wire and board, and the cost of machine, and expense of fencing, puts it within the power of every farmer to enclose his land with the very best and most substantial kind of fencing, at a total cost far below that of any other kind.

Agents Wanted Everywhere.

For prices of machines, and other particulars, call on or address

M. C. HENLEY

Patentee and Manufacturer of Henley's Roller Skates,

FACTORY BUILDING,   **RICHMOND, IND.**
523 to 533 N. Sixteenth St.

A BOY'S COMPOSITION ON RINKS.

Rinks is a new invention. They was invented by Mr. Payne. Rinks is made to skate on. Some people think they were made to fall down on, but they are mistaken. Skating on rinks beats sliding down hill all holler, 'cause you can get so much more slide, and don't have to walk up hill. Girls have more fun skating than boys, 'cause when she falls down all the young men run to help her up, and when a boy falls down they all run and fall down on him. Rinks is more dangerous than mules, 'cause you can stay away from mules, and they won't hurt you; but you can't stay away from them rinks, and they hurt harder than mules sometimes. Next time I go to the rink, I am going to put on my sister's clothes, and then the man with a "soldier's cap" on will hold me up while I skate. It takes lots of get-up-ness to make a good skater. I spend more time getting up than I do skating.

STANDARD MILITARY WORKS.

By Lieut. HUGH T. REED, U. S. Army.

MILITARY SCIENCE AND TACTICS.

Second edition. This work is used as a text-bok at many colleges, and by military men in every State in the Union. It is prepared from the best writings on such subjects as — Single and double rank exercises of a company, Battalion ceremonies, &c., for Infantry; Manual of the piece, &c., for Artillery; School of the trooper, mounted, &c., for Cavalry; Signal codes, Cipher signals, &c., for Signalmen; Target practice; Guard duty; Forms for courts-martial, Boards of survey, Affidavits, Reconnaissance, Military correspondence, &c., all as authorized by the War Department. Also the Articles of War; Constitution of the U.S.; Science and Art of War; Military, Martial and International Law; Field Fortifications; Customs of the Army, Pay, Rations, Cooking Recipes, Clothing; Riots; Volunteers; Militia; List of camp calls; Trumpet music; Forms for morning reports, Programs for competitive drills; Rules for organizing a company, &c., &c. Illustrated. Price, Leather, $3 00.

UPTON'S INFANTRY TACTICS, ABRIDGED.

Second edition. (By permission of the owners of the Copyright of Upton's Tactics.) This work treats only of the Drill, Inspection, &c., of a separate Company, and the forms of all Battalion Ceremonies. It is prepared from the Orders from the War Dept.; Decisions by the late Gen. Upton; Opinions of other Tacticians and Customs of the service on mooted poir.ts. Price, Cloth, 75 cents; Paper, 50 cents.

LIGHT ARTILLERY TACTICS.

Second edition. Compiled from the U. S. Artillery Tactics, and late orders from the War Dept. Gives Manual of the Piece, Mechanical Manœuvres, &c., for field pieces and Gatling guns. Price, Paper, 50 cents.

STANDARD SIGNAL TACTICS.

Second edition. Contains the elements of Military and Naval Signaling used in the United States; gives the General Service Code; Instructions for the Flag, Torch, Lantern, Heliograph, Cipher signals, &c. Illustrated. Price, Cloth, 75 cents.

BROOM TACTICS,

Or Calisthenics in a new form for Young Ladies—Embracing the Schools of the Group and Bevy, Manual of the Broom, Materials for Uniforms, &c. Price, Paper, 25 cents.

Books sent, postpaid, on receipt of price, by

BRENTANO BROTHERS,

101 State St., Chicago, Ill.; 1015 Penn. Ave., Washington, D. C., or 5 Union Square, New York, N. Y.

Printed in Great Britain
by Amazon

60654242R00098